Breaking Out
of the
Darkness

Lynn Baillie

ISBN: 978-1-989506-31-8

Bring your Higher Self in alignment
With your day-to-day actions to create
The future you want most.
-ChildrenofLight

This book is dedicated to you, dear reader. You are my inspiration and reason for writing this book. I know that I am not alone in the things I endured as a child and if I can help you by sharing how I healed my past traumas then I will have accomplished my Divine Purpose. I hope that this book will help you on your journey to healing all that is holding you back from being your true authentic self and introduce you to a life filled with happiness, peace, love, and abundance.

CONTENTS

PREFACE

The task ahead of you
Is never greater than
The strength within you.
— yourpositiveoasis.com

We've all experienced traumatic events throughout our lives; it is a common thread that unites us all as humans. Trauma changes us and can turn once vibrant, happy people into lost, shattered beings consumed by dark thoughts, tragic memories, and unbearable pain.

I've been there. I've suffered unimaginable traumas and, I want to let you know, dear reader, that you are not alone. I can say with certainty that there are things that you have experienced that I have too, and that together, we can heal.

Some of the things I've experienced include sexual abuse by my father, a decade of night terrors from a horrific car accident at two years old, sexual assault by neighborhood boys when I was very young, physical, mental, and emotional abuse from children at school, low self-esteem caused by a parent who was sarcastic and condescending, an attempted drowning by a boy much older than me. All of this led me to have unhealthy relationships with men, women, and people in general. I had a great deal of anxiety around being accepted to the point where I would change my personality to suit my environment and by doing this, caused further harm to myself.

I've also experienced post-natal depression, I almost died giving birth to my son, and my daughter almost died upon delivery. I've been bullied, harassed, and discriminated against in my workplace. My brother died, and so did my mother, under horrible circumstances, and their deaths made an impact on me that is indescribable. I have also endured many physical traumas, such as spinal injury causing bulging discs, degenerative disc disease and stenosis, torn muscles and ligaments, multiple knee surgeries, and concussions. I also have fibromyalgia, and suffer from the pain caused by inflammation daily.

The point of telling you this is not to evoke a feeling of sadness or pity; it's to help you understand that no matter what you've been through, you can heal, just like I did by using the same methods and teachings. With this book, I hope to help encourage you, empower you, and educate you about the transformative power of healing energy and how you can use it to break out of the darkness.

1
LYNN'S STORY

Through others we become ourselves.
— Lev S. Vygotsky

<u>How I discovered Reiki and the Evolution of My Studies</u>

It all began in 2015 when my brother met a psychic lady who apparently had past lives with my family. She ended up being very close with my brother; I'm sure she saved him several times taking his late-night hands-free calls when he was out in his rig hauling various grades of petroleum, including extremely hazardous sour gas, during the extreme winters, at night, in Alberta and British Columbia.

Micki of Muskoka or Psychic Micki was her name in the spirit realm. She worked with the local police helping them to find missing people and she was remarkably effective. In 2015, a three-year-old went missing December twenty fourth and the police knocked at her door. She was packing her things to move to a new house and she paused to help them. They showed her a picture saying the little girl wandered off without her winter coat and could be at risk of freezing to death if not found soon. Within seconds of looking at the picture, Micki described the surroundings of the little girl and said she was hiding behind some crates. With this information the police knew exactly where she was. She had followed her father to work and was hiding behind some pallets. They found the girl five minutes after seeing Micki!

Micki was my inspiration. She told my brother he had a strong ability to heal people and I watched as she showed him how to do it using my mom to practice on. She showed my brother how to ground himself and then call on the spiritually guided life force energy and let it flow from his hands. Micki then showed him how to hold his hands above the area to work on and feel the energy throughout the healing. Once finished they tied a knot in the energy breaking away from my mom's energy, shook their hands to the earth to remove any residual energy from my mom and then put their hands under running tap water to do a final cleanse of the residual energy.

I had no idea this was even possible and was completely intrigued and immediately knew I needed to learn more about how to help people heal. When I asked her if I had the ability to help people heal, she said I did but it wasn't as strong as my brother's. This upset me at first because of my competitiveness but I soon realized I needed to learn more. I went to Micki and asked her to mentor me and help me learn and understand this fascinating world of energy healing.

In 2016, I was living in a condo that had a rooftop pool and the building had a good mix demographically. The retired senior people had their gathering place, and the divorcees had their spot opposite the pool from them. The couples and families in the building intermingled amongst both.

There were a couple of seniors who I enjoyed working with using the Auric Healing method that Micki taught me. One lady had spinal surgery on most of her spine for advanced stenosis. At the base, near her sacrum, it was not repaired, and, as a result, she suffers constant agonizing pain. She has never been free of the pain in the lower part of her spine for many years and somehow after I worked for ten minutes on her lower back with the Auric method Micki taught me she was pain free for three days. It became a regular thing for me to see the lady and help her with her pain. It was exhilarating knowing that I was helping her. As payment, her husband baked me the most amazing pastries. They were absolutely delicious and very much appreciated.

There were others who asked me for some energy healing, and I was happy to help. They were all amazed at how just waving my hands over the area that gave them much pain would make it go away. For some, there was a permanent affect and for others the symptom returned. With my mom, she had a very bad right wrist that she liked to hold her very big coffee mug in. Before I worked on her wrist she couldn't hold a mug of coffee at all. I worked ten minutes one day and went back the next day to see how she was and she still had a bit of an issue and after another ten minutes the pain was gone and it stayed that way for the rest of her days. Soon afterwards I learned reiki and sent it to her whenever I visited and, eventually, every time I was with her, she felt amazing (Normally, she felt the constant burdening effects of her fibromyalgia all over her body). She couldn't believe that just being in the same room with me helped alleviate her pain. When I left, sadly, the effects of the fibromyalgia returned so I visited often.

I learned quickly that auric healing wasn't a commonly understood practice and decided to learn a modality that people recognized or understood that is similar in practice. Reiki fit the search criteria and I learned that many people go to a Reiki practitioner for pain management. This was exactly what I was looking for, and with this knowledge I decided to learn Reiki and find a teacher.

The Reiki Studies Begin

After researching online for a Reiki Teacher, I made a few calls and priced out the courses. There was quite a range of pricing and the most affordable course included healing animals. For me that was a no-brainer. I have always loved working with animals and the teacher wasn't that far from me distance-wise, so I booked the first course. The journey began...

In-person classes

September 30, 2017 – Reiki First Degree in Usui and Animal Reiki System

October 15, 2017 - Reiki Second Degree in Usui and Animal Reiki System

March 18, 2018 – Master Teacher Level in Usui Holy Fire II System

May 11, 2019 – Reiki Tummo Level 1

June 23, 2019 – Reiki Tummo Level 2

June 24, 2019 – Kundalini

August 11, 2019 – Secrets of Natural Walking (SONW) Level 1

September 27, 2019 – Reiki Tummo Level 3a (Personal Mastery)

Online classes

April 25, 2020 - Reiki Tummo Level 1, retake

April 26, 2020 - Reiki Tummo Level 2, retake

May 2, 2020 - Reiki Tummo Level 3a (Personal Mastery), retake

May 3, 2020 - Meditation

June 6, 2020 – Secrets of Natural Healing Level (SONH) 1

June 7, 2020 - Secrets of Natural Healing Level (SONH) 2

July 24, 2020 – Inner Heart Level 1

August 8, 2020 - Secrets of Natural Healing Level (SONH) 3

August 9, 2020 - Secrets of Natural Healing Level (SONH) 4

November 7 & 8, 2020 – Bridging the Heart & Mind level 1

October 4, 2020 – January 3, 2021 – The Priestess Path: Lineages of Light

February 15, 2021 - Energy Medicine: The Secrets of a Master Practitioner, Masterclass

February 18, 2021 – Embrace Your Energy Body, Masterclass

February 21 – April 17, 2021 - Duality

Course descriptions

Reiki First Degree in Usui and Animal Reiki System

Traditional Japanese Reiki meditation techniques are taught and practiced building on energetic knowledge to aid in your own healing process. Energetically clearing and "making whole" creating balance in your life. You receive an attunement to open your energy channel.

Reiki Second Degree in Usui and Animal Reiki System

Expand on First Degree. You learn symbols that help intensify the flow of energy. You have another attunement to help energy flow even better. You learn symbols that help you when channeling energy. You take part in meditations that help build your confidence in working with the life force energy. You learn more about energy healing and that distance and time do not exist in the energy world. This allows you to heal past traumas, perform instantaneous distance healings, and send energy to future events.

Master Teacher Level in Usui Holy Fire II System

The energy of Holy Fire is deeply healing. In the master teacher class, your skills are taken to the next level and far beyond. After completion of this level, Reiki may become a way of life, rather than just a healing therapy. Your body will be ever flowing with this Kundalini energy allowing you to be in alignment with the Universe. At this level, you will feel joy, harmony, and grace in all your experiences.

Reiki Tummo Level 1

In this workshop you learn basic energy channeling/healing for yourself and others. You learn ways to increase your spiritual growth and emotional clearing, how to reduce the effects of stress, unify your mind, body, and soul to ultimately reduce or remove energy blocks and improve your vitality. You also learn a different approach to meditating - you get a different experience when you take a Heart approach.

Reiki Tummo Level 2

In this workshop you improve your connection with the Divine Energy. You learn to activate your Kundalini energy and expand on your healing teachings to be more effective at distance healing, healing others, and healing your environment. All being conducted with a grateful Heart. You learn deeper meditations for better experiences with your Heart as well as to accelerate your Kundalini flow and healing.

Kundalini

By activating your Kundalini energy, you will enhance your Reiki experience. You become more connected to the energy around you and your Chakras will be more developed and easily cleansed. This Kundalini workshop focuses on opening your Heart Chakra because Reiki Tummo is related to working from the Heart. An open and clean Heart will be able to help you heal yourself and others in a much more loving way.

Secrets of Natural Walking (SONW) Level 1

This is a method of walking that activates the energy points on your feet as well as improves your posture. There are many health benefits that were realized by many of the people who took part in this program ranging from pain management to the correction of scoliosis.

Reiki Tummo Level 3a (Personal Mastery)

You receive more attunements to open more Chakras (Throat, Heart, Solar Plexus, Sacral, and Base). The Kundalini fire now reaches at least to your Heart Chakra and a bonus attunement is conducted at the end of the workshop activating your Shing Chi 8 Chakra (1st out of body Chakra above your crown Chakra). The Kundalini energy helps you cleanse your energy body 24/7 – once activated it flows non-stop. You learn how to accelerate the Kundalini cleansing and purifying process so that you can move the core of the Kundalini to higher Chakras.

Secrets of Natural Healing Level (SONH) 1

The goal here is to open your Heart to True Source (God) and surrender all your dreams, hopes, desires, worries, etc., so that you may be free in your Heart from all of those matters and allow yourself to be healed. This will help you feel calmer, more peaceful, and happier in your daily life.

Secrets of Natural Healing Level (SONH) 2

Adding to the teachings of level 1. You take part in more meditations that free your Heart from being burdened by things like your dreams, hopes, desires, worries, etc. You open your Heart more and improve your connection with the Diving Energy.

Secrets of Natural Healing Level (SONH) 3

You learn more about surrendering our wants and interests so that our body and Heart can function more in line with True Source's (God's) will.

Secrets of Natural Healing Level (SONH) 4

During this workshop you have a comprehensive cleanse of all facilities (Chakras, energy channels, connection to Earth, and non-physical body layers). This allows your body to be free naturally and the True Source (God) love can work more completely.

Meditation

You learn how to perform meditation correctly. This workshop includes your pineal gland activation, cleansing and realizing your different body layers, development of your Crown and Heart Chakras to become an instrument for Divine Blessings and energy channel of the Universe.

Inner Heart level 1

This workshop helps you to identify your non-physical heart or Inner Heart. Your Inner Heart is where God or the Divine resides. You will learn to tune into your Inner Heart and let it direct you in a loving way. The more you open your Inner Heart, the stronger the connection.

Bridging the Heart & Mind level 1

Through a series of interactive exercises and meditations, you learn how to strengthen and sustain a more positive state. You learn how to be more resilient and reduce your stress as well as how to be unaffected by negative situations or environments. Ultimately, you learn how to authentically engage with others by smiling, speaking, and listening from the Heart.

The Priestess Path: Lineages of Light

This was a journey to embody the Sacred Priestess Lineages of Light and Devine Feminine Initiations. Many topics are covered, and my favourites were creating sanctuary, how to do ceremony, and meeting your spirit guide(s). It was a very beautiful experience.

Energy Medicine: The Secrets of a Master Practitioner, Masterclass

You learn about your energy system and techniques that help you clear energy blockages. You learn to re-energize yourself, conquer stress, and use energy to choose the right food to eat. This is just a sample of the actual course, and it is, on its own, helpful.

Embrace Your Energy Body, Masterclass

You learn that there is a material/physical world and an energetic world that spans the universe. You learn how to calm your mind so that you can hear your inner voice. You learn the basics of how to activate your creative energy so that you can feel it in the physical world and get a glimpse of how the energy will work for you. You learn how to clear your fears and you learn a bit about manifesting and synchronicity.

I was so impressed by this Masterclass that I signed up for the eight-week class, **Duality**. This class is a more detailed version of Embrace Your Energy Body, Masterclass.

Mikao Usui, is the man who created Reiki in the 1920's in Japan during a mountain meditation retreat in the search for the purpose of life and enlightenment. He sprained his ankle on his mountain journey and realized, through a spiritual awakening, that he could use the energy from his hands to make the pain go away enough for him to finish his journey down the mountain. Usui Reiki was named in his honour.

Meaning of the word Reiki:

Re means "spiritually guided" and Ki means "life force energy" or "Divine energy" and, therefore, Reiki means spiritually guided life force energy. We feel this energy mostly through our hands and it actually flows throughout our body via our energy centers and pathways (i.e., chakras and meridians).

I thoroughly enjoyed learning the above courses and workshops from great mentors and continue to grow my learning. I've read many books and took part in many online webinars about meditation, energy healing, and discovered the many benefits. Read on to find out my continued journey as a student of the energy realm.

2
HEALING MODALITIES
AND
YOUR ENERGY FIELD

Whatever comes, let it come. Whatever stays, Let it stay.
Whatever goes, let it go. – Papaji

Have you ever felt stuck? Perhaps you feel like you're living the same life day after day, year after year. Being stuck is a way of thinking, believing, or doing and is a product of your current emotional state. Remember that you have options, and you don't have to be stuck. Perspective is everything. Happiness, contentment, stillness, belief, and positivity are all possible once we have looked within to see the work we need to do and heal ourselves.

There are many forms of energy healing and although they can vary slightly, the main theme is that the healing power is contained within each of us. The only person who can heal us from within is ourselves. We must be open to the experience and the modality of healing for it to be effective. The forms of energy healing listed below can be used in combination with each other; if we use a broken arm as an example, we enlist a doctor who will recommend a cast to set the broken bone, chiropractic therapy to adjust it, massage to help heal the damaged tissue, and physiotherapy to strengthen it. In all modalities, the practitioner has an interaction with a higher intelligence where this higher intelligence guides the energy throughout the healing process. A person may try multiple modalities to get healed. One on its own or in combination with others may be beneficial. It is your journey to discover what works best for you.

The positive thinker sees the
Invisible, feels the intangible and
Achieves the impossible.
– Winston Churchill

It is possible that some modalities may work better than others. This may not, necessarily, be due to the modality being used but rather the energy level of the practitioner. Not all practitioners are vibrating on the same level – a healer that isn't fully healed themselves vibrates on a lower level. True Masters vibrate at a very high level and are very effective; however, they teach more than they practice. Master Practitioners are working towards that level by practicing and continuous work on themselves. This is me. I am a Master Practitioner and still continue to work on myself with healings and continued learning. I feel that my learning will be ongoing as there is so much to learn. Once you start learning you realize just how much has been kept from us. Information that is extremely useful and beneficial to everyone is available and you just need to be pointed in the right direction to begin your journey of discovering the many benefits of energy healing.

<u>A Few Healing Modalities</u>

Cosmic Energy Healing

Cosmic energy is our purifier, our healer, our true wellness. Sun is responsible for vitamin D synthesis which helps in our overall wellness. It helps us to secrete endorphins, a natural antidepressant. It is possible to bring this cosmic energy to our ecosystem.

Somatic Healing

Somatic healing is a form of body-centered therapy that looks at the connection of mind and body and uses both psychotherapy and physical therapies for holistic healing.

Reiki

Re means "spiritually guided" and Ki means "life force energy" or "Divine energy" and, therefore, Reiki means spiritually guided life force energy. Reiki is the practice of guiding the life force energy to help yourself heal or others to heal. You can send Reiki to past, present, and future experiences as neither time nor distance exist in the energy realm.

Reiki Tummo

Reiki Tummo is founded on Usui Reiki and incorporates the Inner (non-physical) Heart. You learn to use your Inner Heart more in combination with the Reiki, and in doing so, on a daily basis, allows you to achieve true insight and understanding. This compliments the Reiki healing process and makes it a much more loving and effective experience.

Theta Healing (v1)

In the phase of deep meditation, sleep, or hypnosis, the dominant wave is the Theta one and scientists have concluded that this frequency has the ability to lower stress and anxiety, lead to deep relaxation, enhance the mental clarity and creativity, minimize ache, and increase euphoria.

Theta Healing (v2)

This form of Theta Healing was formerly known as Orian Healing and later changed to Theta Healing. This modality uses focused thought and prayer while tapping into the Theta brain wave. This enables us to change the way we think, the way we are, and to program our minds to be better human beings. You connect to the creative energy of All That Is. Changing your beliefs is the major focus of this practice. Your beliefs are what you accumulate over the years – your opinions, your fears, your judgements, the way you think things should be, etc. Theta healing helps you let go of beliefs that are neither useful nor helpful.

Kundalini Power

The Sanskrit term "Kundali Shakti" translates as "Serpent Power". Kundalini is thought to be an energy released within an individual using specific meditation techniques. It is represented symbolically as a serpent coiled at the base of the spine (at your root chakra). By activating your Kundalini energy, you become more connected to the energy around you and your Chakras will be more developed and easily cleansed.

Past Life Regression

Past Life Regression is a method that uses hypnosis to recover what practitioners believe are memories of past lives or incarnations. (I was guided by my spiritual friend through a past life regression. I looked into a mirror and after a period of time I saw how I looked in my past lives. It's fascinating to see a different face looking back at you in the mirror).

Quantum Touch

Quantum Touch is the touch-based healing technique that uses the chi of both practitioner and client, bringing them into harmony to allow the body to heal itself.

EFT (Emotional Freedom Techniques)

EFT is talking through traumatic memories and neutralizing the emotions that are triggered. The practice consists of tapping with your fingertips on specific meridian points.

Restorative Touch

Healing Touch is an energy therapy that uses gentle hand techniques thought to help re-pattern the patient's energy field and accelerate healing of the body, mind, and soul.

Pranic Healing

Pranic Healing is a highly developed and tested system of energy treatment that uses prana to balance, harmonize and transform the body's energy processes. Prana is the Sanskrit word that means life-force. This invisible bioenergy or vital energy keeps the body alive and maintains good health.

Ho'oponopono

Ho'oponopono is a Hawaiian forgiveness ritual, and it is based on oneness or the unity of everything "In all existence". Ho'o means "to make", Pono means "right or correct", Ponopono means "rightly right", and Ho'oponopono means "to make rightly right". To make rightly right means that you join yourself with your higher self and the Source of all Being. In doing so, when you heal something in yourself, then you'll impact your external world and heal its corresponding illness.

Reflexology

Reflexology is based on a theory that specific areas of the feet, hands, and ears, correlate to specific organs and systems in the body. When you apply varying amounts of pressure (massage) to specific points on the feet, hands, and/or ears, it brings relaxation and healing to the corresponding area of the body.

Australian Aboriginal Healing

The world's oldest, sixty-thousand-year-old healing system. It is believed that illness is sourced at the soul level, impacting the physical body. You obtain healing support via the body/mind/soul connection enabling you to discover and reprogram the subconscious motivations behind illness.

Earthing

Another word for earthing is grounding. This is the physical act of connecting your body with the earth. Being barefoot and walking on the earth or having your feet in water allows you access to a source of beneficial energy that counters and frees you from the unwanted energy that builds up from our daily lives.

The Gentle Way

A self-help guide for those who believe in Angels. The Gentle Way shows you how to be in touch with your Guardian Angel on a daily basis following a simple system that results in an easier path in life. Requesting a "Most Benevolent Outcome" (MBO) is asking your Guardian Angel for assistance. You must be specific and exact with your intentions and the desired outcome must be positive and the best for everyone involved.

QiGong

Qi (pronounced "chee") means energy and Gong means something that requires work over a long period of time. As such, QiGong means Energy Work. This is an elegant system of movements that transform and heal your body, mind, and soul. Physically, by doing these fluid movements, you increase your energy, strength, and health.

Secrets of Natural Walking (SONW)

In SONW you learn a method of walking that activates your body's natural self-healing abilities. This method of walking helps correct poor posture, aching joints, and premature aging.

Secrets of Natural Healing (SONH)

Through meditation, SONH helps you to activate your body's self-healing abilities by opening your heart to the Divine energy (True Source) and allowing the Divine blessings to do the work, resulting in a happier and healthier life.

The Silva Mind Control Method

During the Silva Mind Control Method you consciously access altered states of your mind. Alpha, Theta, Delta, and Beta are states of mind where you are able to heal yourself, be creative and find solutions, connect to higher intelligence to remove obstacles, or just be awake.

Open Heart Approach

When you open your heart, you surrender your worries, needs, wants, and desires to True Source to handle in the best possible way for the highest possible good. When you surrender everything to the higher power it allows your heart to be completely free to prioritize that higher power. This will result in a life that is full of love, compassion, and abundance.

The Seven Chakras

Chakra (Sanskrit) means and refers to the energy points in our bodies. They correspond to our nerves, organs, and areas of our bodies that affect our well being both physical and emotional. The Chakra points when they are aligned and open promote health, wellness, happiness, and balance.

Chakra 1: Root Chakra

Location - At the base of the spine and the tailbone area.

Colour - Red

Meaning - Stability, grounding, and physical identity

Blocked Root Chakra - Physical issues can manifest such as arthritis, constipation, bladder, or colon problems. Emotionally we feel insecure about our basic needs being met, we can feel financially insecure, or feel insecure about our well-being.

Open Root Chakra - We will feel grounded and secure, both physically and emotionally when our root chakra is open and aligned.

Chakra 2: Sacral Chakra

Location - Just below the belly button, above the pubic bone

Colour - Orange

Meaning - Creativity, Pleasure, and Sexuality

Blocked Sacral Chakra - Physical issues can manifest such as impotence, lower back pain, and UTI's. This chakra is connected to feelings of our self-worth regarding pleasure, sexuality, and creativity.

Open Sacral Chakra - We feel good about ourselves and open to new ways of being creative and finding pleasure when our sacral chakra is aligned.

Chakra 3: Solar Plexus Chakra

Location - Stomach area, upper abdomen

Colour - Yellow

Meaning - Confidence and Self-esteem

Blocked Solar Plexus Chakra - Physical issues can manifest such as eating disorders, indigestion, heartburn, and ulcers.

Open Solar Plexus Chakra - This is our chakra of personal power and when it is aligned and open, we feel self-confident, and self-assured in who we are.

Chakra 4: Heart Chakra

Location - In the center of the chest, just above the heart

Colour - Green

Meaning - Compassion and Love

Blocked Heart Chakra - Physical manifestations can include weight issues, asthma, and heart problems. Oftentimes this is blocked because of putting others' needs before our own. When out of alignment, we will feel isolated, lonely, and insecure.

Open Heart Chakra - The heart chakra bridges the lower and upper chakras and when open and aligned it represents our ability to connect with and love others.

Chakra 5: Throat Chakra

Location - The throat

Colour - Blue

Meaning - This chakra is connected to communication, self-expression, and truth.

Blocked Throat Chakra - Voice and throat problems as well as thyroid, teeth, gums, and jaw issues can manifest when the throat chakra is blocked. Gossip, interrupting, and dominating the conversation can cause blockages as well as feeling like you've lost your ability to voice your opinions.

Open Throat Chakra - When the throat chakra is open, we speak our truth, and we listen with compassion. We say what needs to be said and are confident in our words.

Chakra 6: Third Eye Chakra

Location - On the forehead between the eyes

Colour - Indigo

Meaning - Intuition, Inner guidance, Imagination

Blocked Third Eye Chakra - Blockages can manifest as headaches, migraines, hearing issues, and vision problems. People who are know-it-alls or those who are out of touch with their intuition have blockages in this chakra.

Open Third Eye Chakra - The ability to see the big picture and the ability to follow our intuition and inner guidance happens when the chakra is open and aligned.

Chakra 7: Crown Chakra

Location - The very top of the head

Colour - White or Violet

Meaning - Intelligence and awareness, connection to awareness and life's purpose

Blocked Crown Chakra - When the crown chakra is blocked it manifests in skepticism, narrow-mindedness, suspicion, and stubbornness.

Open Crown Chakra - When this chakra is open (because it is connected to all other chakras) we are said to be enlightened and blissful.

You will know if your Chakras are blocked if you are feeling stress, sluggish, pain, stiffness, chaotic, unsettled, and insecure.

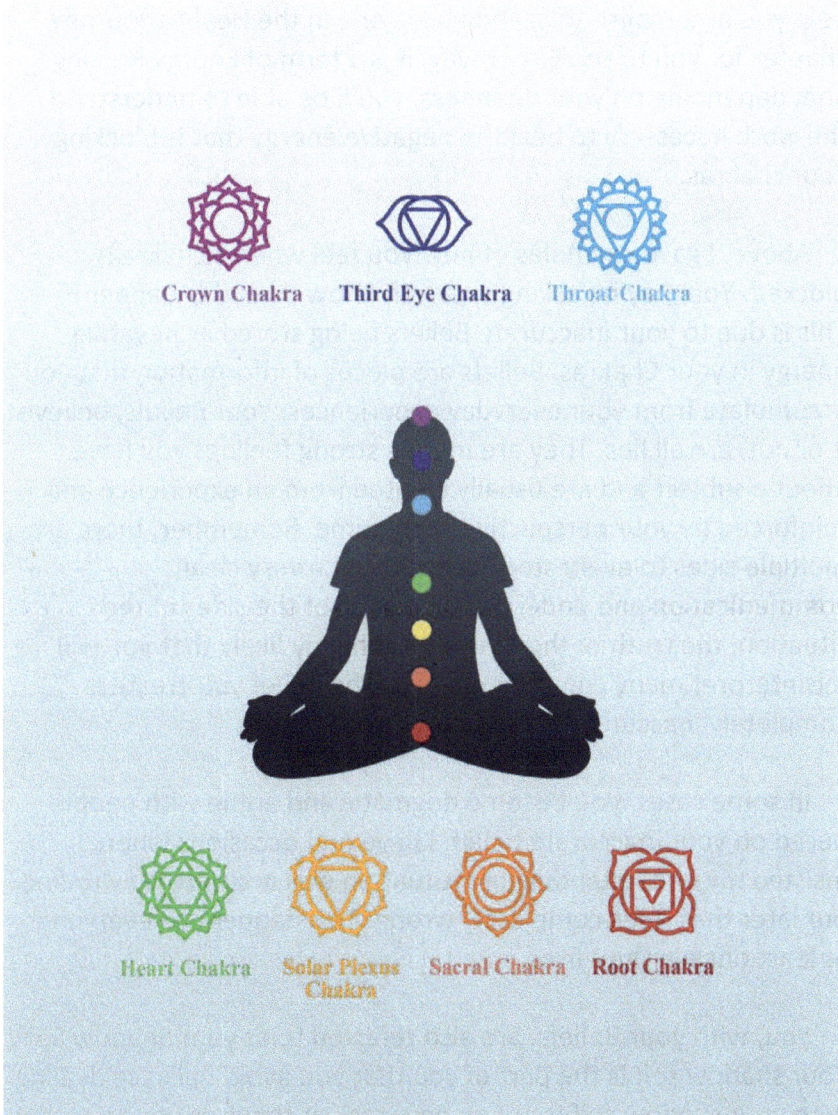

Crown Chakra   Third Eye Chakra   Throat Chakra

Heart Chakra   Solar Plexus Chakra   Sacral Chakra   Root Chakra

Unblocking a chakra is clearing it of negative energy or misinformation. You can have a Reiki Practitioner, who specializes in chakra work, help you remove the blockages, or you can do the work on yourself. There are guided meditations online that can help you accomplish this, and I have one in the Healing Journey chapter for you to try. Either way, it is a form of Energy Healing and, depending on your openness, you'll be able to understand the work necessary to heal the negative energy that is blocking your chakras.

Above, I gave examples of how you feel when a chakra is blocked. You may be asking yourself, "How does this happen?" This is due to your inaccurate Beliefs being stored as negative energy in your Chakras. Beliefs are pieces of information that you accumulate from your everyday experiences. Your Beliefs, believe it or not, are all lies. They are merely strong feelings you have about a subject and are usually created from an experience and reinforced by your perspective at the time. Remember, there are multiple sides to every story and without a very clear communication and understanding of all of the sides of the situation, the truth of the matter, it is highly likely that you will misinterpret many components of it. The Belief you create is completely inaccurate and stored in your Chakra.

In some cases, you become dogmatic and argue with people based on your inaccurate belief. I have had occasions where I insisted my understanding of a situation was accurate only to find out later that I was completely wrong. This happens to everyone at least once in their lives.

You, with your Beliefs, are also referred to as your Shadow Self. Your shadow self is the part of you that you avoid because dealing with your shadow self is not an easy task. It requires you to accept your darkness. You are facing truths about yourself that are difficult to accept. Through self love you will be able to work through that darkness and clear it out of your shadow. You may always have a shadow self. Embrace it, love it, and be mindful. This will help you be more in your light than in your shadow.

The most fundamental aggression to ourselves, the most fundamental harm we can do to ourselves, is to remain ignorant by not having the courage and the respect to look at ourselves honestly and gently.
— Pema Chödrön

The Shadow Self

Your shadow self is a reflection of your imperfect self that needs work. If you want peace, then you must deal with your junk; don't deny dealing with your Shadow Self. When you find that people irritate you, then this reflects something in yourself that needs work. If you do the work, you will be able to live consciously; being aware of your Shadow Self and feeling more clearly.

Until you make the unconscious conscious, it will direct your life and you will call it fate.
— Carl Jung

Shadow work is when you change your perspective from *why me?* To *what am I learning from this?*

If you are in a relationship where you are trying to be someone other than your true authentic self, then you are living in your shadow. We start from birth learning how to please others. Our parents are the first exposure to behaving in such a way that pleases them. Unless you are encouraged from a very young age to be your true authentic self, by your parents and immediate family influencers, you may fall into the cycle of negative feelings and experiences.

When you realize that you are living in your shadow, you can make changes. Changing your perspective is a big one. When with your friends and loved ones or even colleagues try this:

- ❖ Be aware and ask yourself, "How do I wish to perceive them?";
- ❖ Be aware and ask yourself, "How do I wish them to perceive me?"; and
- ❖ Be neutral and have no expectations.

Replace "I should be…" with "I am…" I am that I wish to show and that I wish to be seen. Be authentic. Be you.

Design your life in a 5D (5th density) way by:

- ❖ Eating healthy;
- ❖ Exercise;
- ❖ Interact with people in a loving way;
- ❖ Become your higher self; and
- ❖ Being a complimentary Being in situations to create a positive feedback loop.

The things that bog us down and slow our growth are our beliefs that create our shadow self and until you address those beliefs and see them for what they really are, you will not be able to be the best you can be. We are all here to experience and evolve. When you shine your light bright from within, the shadow will no longer be able to form and you will become your true authentic self. Once you are your true authentic self, you will attract abundance in everything.

The Aura

The word "aura" comes from the Latin word meaning GOLDEN or the Greek word meaning AIR or WIND. The Aura is also called the Electromagnetic Field or the Human Energy Field.

The aura can be many colours, typically the chakra colours, as well as white, gold, silver, grey, brown, and black. The colours are usually stronger around the head than around the body. These colours can vary in brightness and resemble a rainbow after a storm or the flowing northern lights. The aura is created by the combination of the magnetic field, electric field, ultraviolet radiation, hormonal and chemical secretions, and spiritual energy.

Each colour has a meaning similar to what was explained above in relation to the chakras. There are good/positive colours and bad/negative colours.

Positive colours are pure and clear laminations of energy and are very beautiful.

- ❖ Light blue – peaceful, loving, and spiritual - teacher or counselor;
- ❖ Mid-blue – practical and business oriented - technical writers, technicians, computer analysts, engineers, scientists, medical doctors;
- ❖ Dark blue – very creative and artistic - writers, artists;
- ❖ Light to mid-green – natural healers - nurse, medical doctor, counsellor, massage therapist;
- ❖ Sunshine or light yellow – positive and outgoing - comedians, extroverts, true optimist;
- ❖ Baby pink – deep universal love for humankind, give of themselves to help others – counsellor, social workers, volunteers; and
- ❖ Medium to dark red (burgundy) – sexual energy and quite lusty in nature.

Neutral colours are neither good nor bad.

❖ Honey or golden brown – earthly materialistic energy, power, wealth, and social position – executives, accountants, wealthy merchants, politicians, lawyers.

Rare Positive colours have a very high vibration and represent true enlightenment.

❖ White – highest vibration, contains all colours and more – on your true path or about to enter it;
❖ Gold – wisdom and knowledge from a higher source or dimension - highly intuitive, very perceptive, heightened awareness;
❖ Silver – psychic and spiritual awakening – people who are realizing their purpose in life;
❖ Light purple – combination of psychic abilities and spiritual enlightenment – intuitive counsellors, teachers, and advisors;
❖ Mid purple – psychic gifts – you are able to use your intuition to seek answers for yourself and others; and
❖ Light to mid orange – creative humor – witty story tellers.

Negative colours are undesirable colours that represent negative emotions such as fear, guilt, anger, jealousy, worry, and/or sadness. Minor illnesses also affect your energy field making the colours cloudy or unpleasant to look at.

❖ Black – the exact opposite of white – the bigger the problem, the darker the black;
❖ Gray – same as black but not as bad;
❖ Dirty yellow – energy blocks that result in health problems;
❖ Dirty orange – same as dirty yellow but not as bad;
❖ Dull brown – low ethical standards;
❖ Dirty brown – indicates cancer or near death;
❖ Bright pink (pastel baby pink mixed with a harsh red) – soft

brightness with angry intensity – argumentative people;

❖ Light red – anger, frustration, and/or energy blocks – could lead to heart conditions;

❖ Reddish purple – psychic abilities and anger – being angry and break a glass by telekinesis; and

❖ Dark green – jealousy or envy of others.

What do you think your aura looks like?

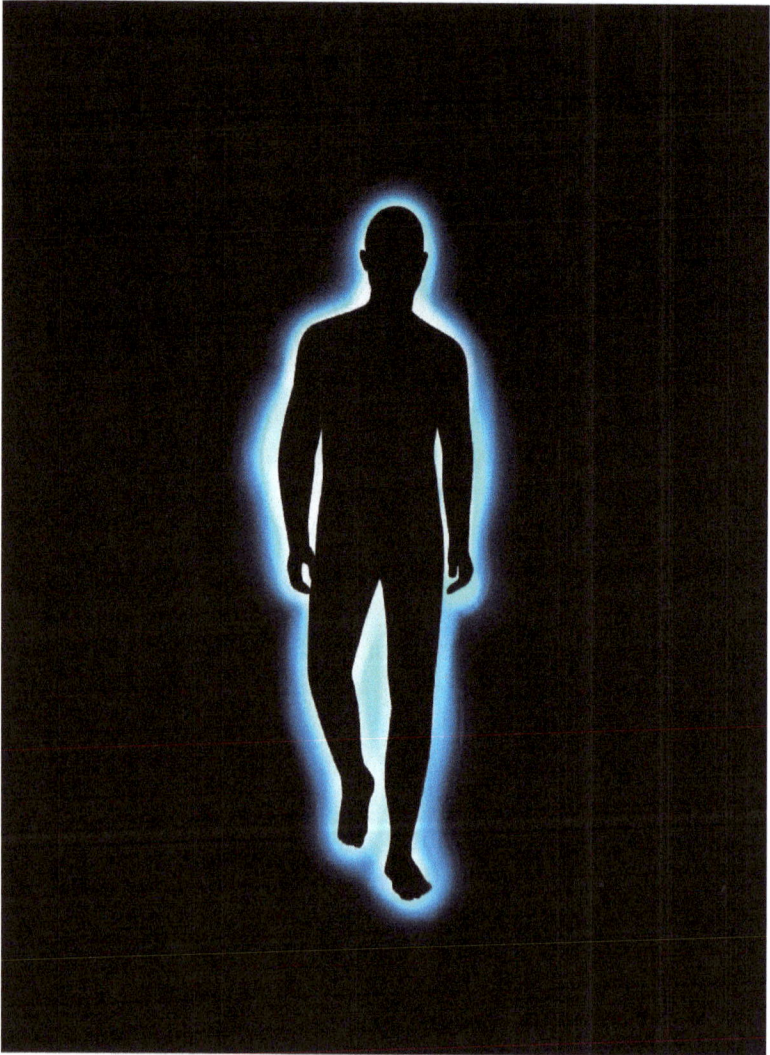

The TORUS Energy Field

A torus is basically the shape of a donut with a hole in the center; only the hole in the torus field is infinitely small. We have a torus field (electromagnetic field) around our body and a smaller torus field around our heart. All matter has energy and, as such, has a torus field around it. There is a cycle related to this torus energy and is easier to visualize if we are in a standing position. Energy comes from above us and enters at our crown chakra, flows through our body to the earth where it is reflected and flows back up into us. As it goes up through our body, it activates our energy centers (chakras) along the way. When the energy reaches the crown chakra it is released and then it flows like a perfectly circular fountain in all directions and circles down to the root chakra. This energy continuously flows in this pattern creating a cycle or the Torus flow and is replenished by the constant cosmic steam of energy entering the crown chakra.

It is possible for the Torus field to be out of balance and this imbalance may have a physical impact on you. Negative energies in your field cause this imbalance and create a situation where the law of cause and effect becomes an issue for you. When you emit these negative energies, you attract that same energy back and this may create cycles/loops of bad relationships and possibly illness.

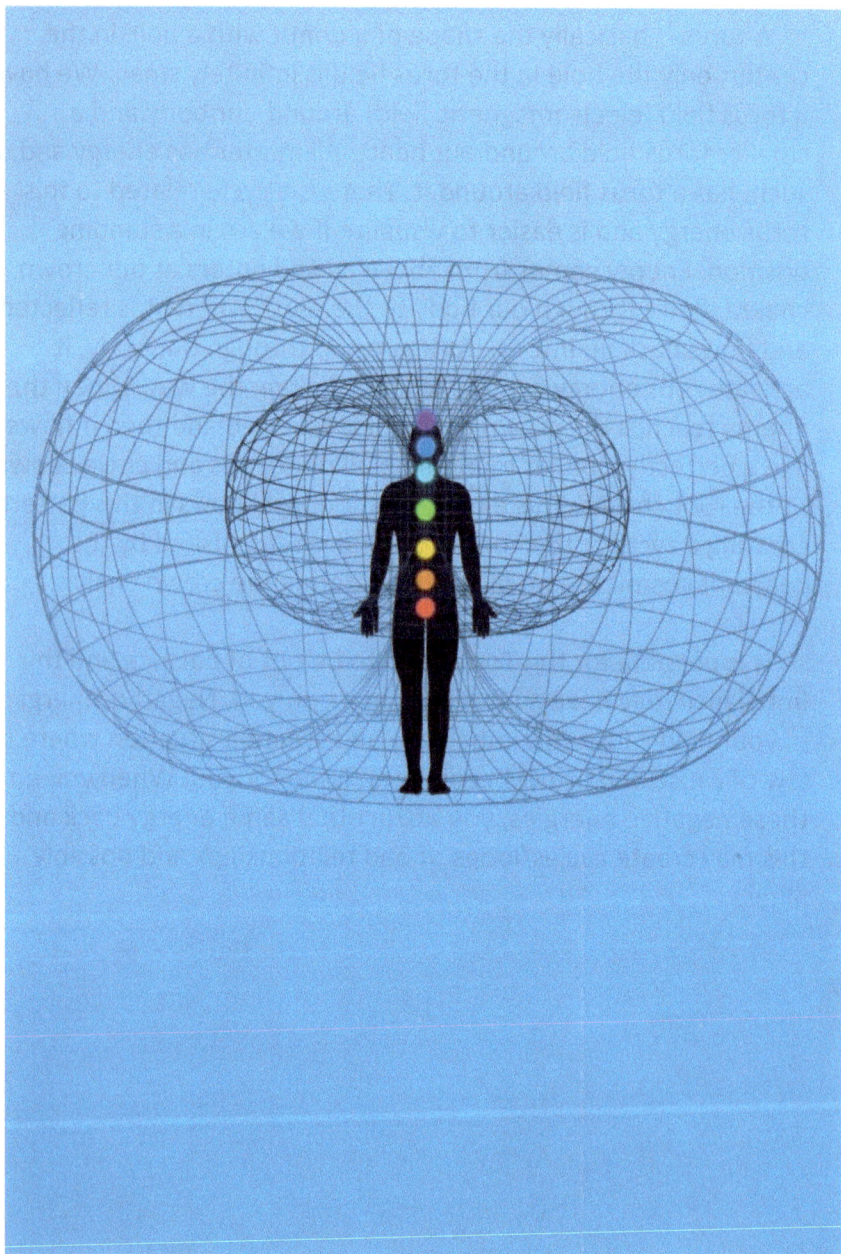

There are many methods for looking inward and facing what is holding you back from being your True Authentic Self. Working on your Beliefs or Shadow Self is a great place to begin. Look at your beliefs and see if they are actually helpful. If they are not helpful, then let them go. The more beliefs you can let go, the clearer your world will become. Changing your perspective is another move in the positive direction. Having a neutral perspective allows you to see the truth in each situation and you will have a more beneficial outcome every time. You will find that you are happier and more content. You may even find that your world flows much better, and you have more synchronicities as if you are connected to the energies of the Universe.

> *Looking at beauty in the world, is the first step of*
> *purifying the mind.*
> — Amit Ray

3
LAWS OF THE UNIVERSE

Travel light. Live light. Spread
The light. Be the light.
– Yogi Bhaj

When I was a child, I felt that I was a part of something bigger than our current physical reality. It was more of a feeling or a knowing and as I grew and was influenced by my family, friends, schoolteachers, news, and social media, I lost my connection to that reality. The more society influenced me, the less connected I became. If these laws had been incorporated into our upbringing, our world would be conflict-free and very prosperous. It boggles my mind why these laws have been kept from us. They are simple and easy to understand and if we all follow them, then there will be much love and abundance for all.

Laws of the Universe

Law of Divine Oneness

We are all connected to each other through creation. Everything we do impacts the collective and has a ripple effect. This is the Supreme Law of all the laws.

Law of Vibration

Everything is always in motion and is either being pushed away or pulled toward something. Similar vibrations are attracted to each other.

Law of Correspondence

Our lives are created by the subconscious patterns that we repeat every single day and they either help us or hinder us.

Law of Attraction

The law of vibration in action. This law is a clear mirror of our self-worth and mindset. We attract what we think about most of the time.

Law of Inspired Action

Take action in order to bring what you want to fruition. Take the necessary steps to get what you desire. This law is often left out when studying the Law of Attraction, but it's one of the most important pieces to the puzzle. Also known as the Law of Action.

Law of Perpetual Transmutation of Energy

Even the smallest action can have a profound effect. You have the power within you to move mountains and small shifts can bring about massive results.

Law of Cause and Effect

Any action causes a reaction, and you get back what you put out. Be aware of how your actions and decisions affect you and everyone around you.

Law of Compensation

Reaping what you sow. You will be compensated for what you do, not always financially, but for all your contributions to the world around you and if you are open to receive the many ways the universe compensates you, you will be repaid with joy, happiness, and peace.

Law of Relativity

Nothing is either good or bad. There is a spectrum of expression and there is always more than one perspective.

Law of Polarity

Everything has a polar opposite, and one cannot exist without the other. Every stage of life has tremendous gifts to offer. Without sickness, we would not know health, etc.

Law of Perpetual Motion

Everything is forever changing, and our job is to embrace the ride. This is important to be grateful in the moment and to realize that things will always change.

Law of Giving and Receiving

Giving and receiving need to be in balance. Some of us find it hard to receive, but when we say no thank you to help or gifts from others, we are blocking their opportunity to follow this law and their chance to experience the wonderful feelings that come from giving.

The Law of Rhythm

Also known as the Law of Flow. This law determines cycles, stages, patterns, and seasons in All things. In cycles, for example, there are highs and lows. To avoid the lows or minimize the impact of the lows, remain positive, persevere, and be consistent in your higher vibration.

What we think, we create;
What we feel, we attract;
and what we imagine, we become.
- Adele Bashere

Universal Law

Cause no harm

What we say and do can harm others and it's important that we remember this. Harm can include gossip, guilt trips, manipulation, and competition. Speak and act from a place of love and compassion.

Cause no loss

When we take things from others, we are causing loss in their lives. Taking things from others often leads to us feeling emptier than before we took it.

Do no damage

Damage comes in all different forms such as destructive

patterns, physical and mental damage, damage of reputation, and emotional damage such as giving someone the silent treatment. The way we speak to and treat others as well as the actions we take should not be damaging.

Don't impose your will on others

Trying to control others by any means is very harmful. Allow others to be as they are, accept them fully and understand that you do not need to make them see things from your point of view, or try and get them to agree with what you believe. Let others be and follow their own divine path.

Awareness

Your level of awareness (density or vibration) is directly related to your alignment with these laws. The higher the level of awareness, the more you live in accordance with these laws.

1st Density

Elements such as earth, rock, water, air, etc., are elemental energies called First Density materials. First Density is the density of Being. Wind blowing over mountains and causing erosion and water crashing onto rocks and onto sandy beaches are examples of First Density and Being. These materials do not have a sense of consciousness. They simply are. And although they are made up of vibrations just as we are, they do not have awareness.

2nd Density

Animals, and plants experience engagement and interaction with others and the world around them. Wolves are an excellent example with pack mentality and where relationships are essential for survival. The relationship is instinctual and may have a hierarchy, but there is a shared identity and single consciousness for the survival of the pack as a whole. Still, the wolves understand that they are individuals aside from their involvement with the pack.

3rd Density

Third Density is the density of self-awareness. There is a separation of us and the world. It's a process of becoming awake. It is consciousness enveloped in a body and an ability to think for and be aware of itself. It is I AM. It is me vs. you and where we decide if we will serve others or serve ourselves. Service to self is much about domination and enslavement of others. Service to others is about sharing, love, kindness, empathy, and generosity. We are allowed to choose, and Third Density is about free will.

4th Density

Fourth Density is about love, compassion, and understanding with the awareness that we are all one. We want to feel connection to other beings through relationships, service to others and inseparability. Love and service to others is the main concept in Fourth Density.

5th Density

Fifth Density is where we teach ourselves the lessons of independence and wisdom. We realize that everything exists inside our Consciousness. We know that there is no world outside ourselves and that we are all one. Everything is contained within the individual. This is the density of Light, or Wisdom.

6th Density

Sixth Density is the density where your Higher Self or your soul lives. It is an awareness of your energy and light and that you are not contained to a specific space, place, or time.

7th Density

In 7th Density, the Consciousness is experienced through millions of years of evolution. There is a sense of completion of wisdom and love and the balance contained therein and has now made itself available to all creation. There is a pull back to Source. This is collective consciousness, one infinite creator, and beyond everything and all that is. This is transcension and infinity.

Our Guides

In the 5th density we learn that we are all one. I am you and you are me. We are connected to all the energy in the universe. Some people call our guiding energy or 6th density, Angels, Spirit Guides, your Higher Self, or Ancestors. For example, your intuition is your higher self or Angels guiding you. We can't see them, but we know they are there and there is a scientific reason why we cannot see them.

It has been said that our guides are already among us, and we can't see them due to their higher vibration. Their frequency is outside what human eyes can detect. We only see a small percentage of the light spectrum and that is the visible light from 390-700nm. In the following, from left to right, the frequency increases or the wavelength decreases: Radio waves (300GHz) – TV – Microwaves – infrared radiation – *visible light (380-700nm)* – Ultraviolet radiation – X-rays – Gama rays – cosmic rays ($10^{\wedge}$ (-10) um or micrometer or 0.0000000001um). [1GHz = 1,000,000,000Hz, 1Hz = 400nm, and 1nm = 1000um.] You can see how broad the spectrum is and that we can only see a very small fragment of it. We have the ability to see many things and knowing that there is much that we aren't seeing helps us to understand that just because we can't see them doesn't mean that they aren't there.

It is entirely possible that other worldly Beings are among us that we cannot see, and they are not here to physically interact, but rather guide us on our Divine Path. Some of us see them and/or hear them, others can feel their presence, and many are completely unaware or uninterested. Only those who are ready for the 'interaction' are able to understand it. Most people are currently living in third density reality (unaware or asleep or unawakened) and in this state we cannot see beyond the visible light. When we get to the fourth density reality, we begin to see, hear, and experience things on a more connected spiritual level (awakened) and have the potential to see beyond what is normally the visible light. The fifth density is where we have evolved and are in the world without all our past mental and emotional traumas. We are our pure true selves. In this dimension, there are no negative emotions or judgement. There is no suffering or sense of loss. In this density we have an even stronger potential to see beyond the visible light.

The Universe is vast, energetic, and very loving. As our guides help us to find our divine paths and we evolve into our higher densities, the laws will become second nature to us. We, as a collective consciousness, are evolving together and moving away from fear-based living and towards a loving existence, a very prosperous and abundant way of life.

Often, it's the deepest pain which empowers you to grow into your higher self. Change is inevitable, but transformation is by conscious choice. Beautiful are those whose brokenness gives birth to transformation and wisdom.
– Tiffinity Art

4
SUPPORTING SCIENCE

Quantum physics thus reveals a basic oneness of the universe.
– Erwin Schrodinger

Have you ever wondered how we got here; How we managed to be on Earth, one tiny planet in the vast universe? Do you wonder how the planets stay in orbit and the stars are always where you expect them to be? What allows the rays of the sun to travel to Earth? What is the glue that holds everything together? There are so many questions...

It was once thought that the world was flat and as technology improved, we were able to see and understand that the world is round and part of a vast evolving and expanding universe. Currently, most believe that we are all individuals living separate lives and that our thoughts and actions only help or harm ourselves and/or our immediate surroundings. Due to some experiments conducted not too long ago, it has been determined that our way of thinking is not entirely correct. We are more connected than we have been made to believe. Science has shown that we live in an entangled and holographic universe and that our actions, thoughts, and words matter.

We are all connected...
Everything is entangled or connected to everything else.

The twin photon experiment

This phenomenon was observed during a quantum physics experiment in CERN in 1982 by physicist David Bohm where a photon was split into two particles and then placed 14km apart. The experiment was conducted to see what would happen if an action was applied to one of the two particles. Surprisingly, upon applying an action upon one particle the other particle, immediately and simultaneously responded in the exact same manner as the particle being acted upon. This connectivity is called quantum entanglement, and this means what once was connected remains connected even though the parts may no longer be physically connected. Einstein called this, "spooky action at a distance." Although they are no longer physically connected, they remain energetically entangled and remain forever instantaneously influenced by each other.

If you take this information and look back at the Big Bang, you see an even larger entanglement. The Big Bang is the idea that the Universe began as a single point and with a Big Bang it expanded to what it is today. Starting from a single point is very relevant here and if you apply the findings of the experiment above you will see that everything in the Universe is entangled. Everything, everywhere, in all existence is connected on a quantum level.

These findings brought David Bohm to believe that

independent reality as we currently know it does not exist and even though the universe appears to be made up of separate parts it is actually a gigantic, entangled, and intricately detailed hologram.

We Live in a Holographic Universe

A hologram is a 3D image created by shining a light beam through a 2D image that has a special property. If you cut the 2D image into pieces and look at the smallest piece under a microscope you will see the exact same image as the original image. In fact, all the images on each of the cuttings will be identical to the original 2D image.

This phenomenon was illustrated by cutting up a holographic bookmark with the smallest piece being difficult to detect without looking under a microscope. The results were remarkable. No matter which piece you looked at, they all had the exact same 2D image on them. The original bookmark had the same image as the smallest piece. A simple definition by Paul Lenda states, "Within a hologram, the whole is within the part. No matter how many times you divide the whole, the part will always contain its totality."

I also like the way that Gregg Braden explains the Holographic principle. "A pattern that is whole and complete unto itself and at the same time it's part of an even greater pattern that is whole and complete unto itself while at the same time is part of an even greater pattern... and so on..." "If you make a change to any part of the hologram, it is mirrored throughout the hologram."

David Bohm concluded that we must live in an entangled and holographic universe based on his twin photon experiment. The analogy with the Big Bang further supports that all matter and everything in between is energetically connected. Science supports that being separate and independent is no longer our reality and, as such, we are infinitely connected with all that is in our universe on an energetic level. This applies to non-physical energy, physical matter, and even our cells are holographic in nature and means that the smallest molecules of our bodies are connected to the smallest molecules in nature.

Consciousness also works in this entangled and holographic manner which means we are part of a Unity Consciousness. We must be mindful of what we say, think, and do because being connected on a conscious level means that our actions, thoughts, and words will have a ripple effect throughout the universe. What impact do you want to make?

The quantum field is...
An invisible field of energy and information that exist beyond
Space and time. Nothing physical or material exists there.
It's beyond anything you can perceive with your senses.
This unified field of energy and information
Is what governs all the laws of nature.
– Dr. Joe Dispenza

The Effect of Human Consciousness on Reality

An experiment was conducted by Dr. Masaru Emoto where he put water into different jars and labeled them hate, ignore, stupid, etc., and others were labelled love, thank you, etc. He studied the positive and negative effects of applying these energies on the water. What he found was fascinating! Under the microscope, he found that the jars with the positive emotions directed at the water, that once frozen, crystallized into beautiful harmonious patterns and the jars with the negative emotions directed at the water, after being frozen, all had horribly misshapen crystallization. This is an example of how The Law of Cause and Effect works in the real world. Your thoughts and words are made of energy and have a resonating impact on all that is.

The Effect of Conscious Intention on Human DNA

In mind-body medicine you generate mental images and direct them at the body with intention resulting in profound physiological changes. In some instances, it has been found that tumor growth was stopped and even reversed.

Focused intention has been studied in both physical and biological systems. QiGong practitioners have been studied and found that their focused intention has a biological effect. Their intention is to heal or normalize the state of health.

Different intentions have different biological effects and there have been studies comparing goal directed healing and qualitative healing. Goal directed is when you apply a specific intention and qualitative healing is when you do not have an intention and surrender the healing to God. These two states of consciousness produce very different effects.

Quantum physics tells us that nothing
that is observed is unaffected by the observer.
That statement, from science, holds an enormous
And powerful insight. It means that everyone sees
A different truth, because everyone is creating what they see.
– Neale Donald Walsh

Effects of Intentionality on DNA Synthesis in cultured tumor cells

In this study the healer, in one room, focused on three petri dishes and a non-healer in a different room had three petri dishes with them. The healer sent three intentions to the petri dishes in his room and the non-healer read a book so as not to interact with the petri dishes in his room. The number of cancer cells in each of the dishes were measured prior to the initial intentions and afterwards the petri dishes were treated and set aside and allowed to grow for twenty four hours. The petri dishes were blind labeled for the next step where the healer used conscious meditation to send five different intentions to the petri dishes. Conscious meditation was performed so that intentional focusing and cohering of energy were possible.

The five intentions are:

1)   Returning the cells to their natural order (prior to being cancerous);
2)   Circulating the microcosmic orbit (Taoist QiGong energy cultivation technique);
3)   Letting God's will flow through the healer's hands (transpersonal intention);
4)   Unconditional love (no direction to the energy);
5)   Dematerialization into the light or into the void.

In all five intentions the healer felt genuine unconditional love and this allowed them to be at the same vibration as the cells that they were sending intentions to. Each intention had a different biological response. Three of the above intentions (1, 2, and 3) had a positive impact on the tumor cells. For the first intention, 39% of the tumor cells were brought back to normal or to their natural order. God's will was half as effective at 21% improvement. In the microcosmic state of consciousness, the cancer cell growth was inhibited by 18%, and unconditional love had no effect. The opposite was found to be true. When the intention of an increase in the number of tumor cells was sent to the petri dish there was a 15% increase in growth. The study also found that using intention alone or imagery alone was half as effective as using them both together. Alone each had a 20% benefit and together they had 40% benefit.

The conclusion was that DNA synthesis was dependent on the intention of the healer, different intentions produced different biological effects, and adding imagery to the intention doubled the impact.

Effect of Intentionality on the DNA Helix

In one study, the body's electromagnetic (EM) field was measured by an Electrocardiogram (ECG) while in positive emotional states. The ECG measures the patterns of the coherent frequency of the emotions of individuals. They also found that the ECGs with the positive emotions were related to enhanced immune systems. The coherent EM radiating from the heart of those in a state of love are typically healthy. The assumption is that the DNA of the cancer cells acts as antennae receiving the energy fields of the heart from the healer causing physiological changes in the cellular health of the cancer cells. This means that the coherent bio-fields of the heart of the healer are considered to regulate the healing process of the receiving cells.

In another study, DNA was extracted and put in an aqueous solution in a beaker and placed in front of the individual who would intend to change the DNA. The unwinding and winding of the DNA was measured in this experiment. Unwinding DNA means that the cell is preparing to divide and winding of DNA means that the DNA is healing or repairing.

A combination of intention, unconditional love, and focused imagery were directed at the DNA molecule focusing on the hydrogen bonds that hold the two strands together. Different intentions had different effects on the winding or unwinding of the DNA.

The energetic connection between the heart intention of the healer and the DNA was measured by ECG. ECGs that had a coherent measurement were in those who were better able to resonate with the DNA and effect changes. Those with an incoherent ECG pattern were unable to effect change in the DNA.

When feeling unconditional love focusing on their heart and no focused intention at the DNA the result was a zero effect on the DNA. Therefore, the healer's coherent energy fields (genuine loving feeling from the heart) combined with a specific intention, when directed at an organ, cell, or metabolic pathway, had a healing effect.

Further experiments were conducted to show that at a distance the above was also possible. The heart has both electromagnetic and non-electromagnetic fields. The non-electromagnetic field is what carries the heart energy field and intention over the distances. This explains why energy healers can heal from distances of thousands of miles.

Learn how to see.
Realize that everything
connects to everything else.
– Leonardo da Vinci

An experiment where a person in California sent an intention to a petri dish in Russia was conducted. The time and duration of the experiment were decided in advance. A thirty-minute window was used and the petri dish with DNA in it was measured and set out at the precise time agreed upon. The results were measured against a control group and found that the DNA showed increased winding or repairing. This test was conducted by known energy healers, they had different techniques but all of them used a heart focused approach. Of the group of energy healers, at least two were able to generate ECG coherence and positively influenced the DNA. In order to effect change in the DNA the healer must be able to generate ECG coherence, and this is possible by coming from a true and sincere place of unconditional love combined with focused intention.

Effect of Intentionality on the Electrical Properties of DNA

An electrical current was introduced to a solution containing DNA. Ions from the DNA were released into the solution and bonded to the electrodes of the mechanism creating the electrical current. How the ions bonded to the electrodes indicated the charge of the DNA molecule. Skin cells were also tested simultaneously in real time and compared to the DNA results.

Throughout the experiment there were positive and negative energy spikes and no response in some instances. This indicated that there was an impact on the DNAs electrical energy by the human intentions. Different intentions had different changes in the DNAs electrical response. When the experimenters had highly charged emotional conversations there were large amplitude spikes in the measured electrical energy of the DNA. In some cases, the DNA was affected and not the skin cells and vice versa. When the conversation was about genetic engineering the DNA responded, and the skin cells did not and when the subject was about nutrition and diet the skin cells responded and the DNA did not. This means that when healing specific parts of your body or specific systems in the body, the intention must be one that resonates best with the DNA of that part of the body or system.

Based on the experiments, conscious intention can influence DNA replication, the winding and unwinding of the DNA helix, and the electrical properties of DNA. In the ancient teachings, the conscious intention of the energy healers was to restore the cells to their natural order or to the state of perfect health. It is no surprise that this was the conscious intention that had the greatest effect on the DNA and cell health. This further sends us a strong message that mere thoughts have an energetic impact on a cellular level and, therefore, on yourself and your surroundings. Your words and actions are no longer your primary concern. Your thoughts must be in check as well. Always be kind, compassionate, and love unconditionally. By directing this energy at yourself and radiating it outward, you will have a positive impact on your wellbeing and all that is around you.

If your compassion does not include yourself, it is incomplete.
— Buddha

From the Bible

The following references are from the online New International Version (NIV) of the Bible and are included in this book to show that the Divine Connection we see in the Bible is similar to the Divine Connection in the realm of energy healing. All energy healers call on the Creator energy of the Universe to flow through them or be directed by them to help heal those in need. Some of the names of the Creator of all that is are God, Jesus, Christ, Buddha, Shiva, Allah, Goddess, Yahweh, Gaia, The Tao, Divine Source, The Source, or True Source. I tend to interchange God, Divine Source, and True Source when explaining energy healing.

The first three quotes are not about healing but are about my journey. The Golden Rule is self-explanatory and Matthew 7:7 is about me asking for Divine help to attune my chakras and to heal my shattered soul. Proverbs 16:24 is a reminder to live in gratitude.

Matthew 7:12 - The Golden Rule - So in everything, do to others what you would have them do to you, for this sums up the Law and the Prophets.

Matthew 7:7 - Ask and it will be given to you; seek and you will find; knock and the door will be opened to you.

Proverbs 16:24 - Gracious words are a honeycomb, sweet to the soul and healing to the bones.

Isaiah 58:8 - Then your light will break forth like the dawn, and your healing will quickly appear; then your righteousness will go before you, and the glory of the Lord will be your rear guard.

Matthew 9:35 - Jesus went through all the towns and villages, teaching in their synagogues, proclaiming the good news of the kingdom, and healing every disease and sickness.

Matthew 10 - Jesus called his twelve disciples to him and gave them authority to drive out impure spirits and to heal every disease and sickness.

Luke 9 - When Jesus had called the Twelve together, he gave them power and authority to drive out all demons and to cure diseases.

Luke 9:11 - but the crowds learned about it and followed him. He welcomed them and spoke to them about the kingdom of God, and healed those who needed healing.

1 Corinthians 12:28 - And God has placed in the church first of all apostles, second prophets, third teachers, then miracles, then gifts of healing, of helping, of guidance, and of different kinds of tongues.

1 Corinthians 12 - Spiritual Gifts - Now about the gifts of the Spirit, brothers and sisters, I do not want you to be uninformed. **2** You know that when you were pagans, somehow or other you were influenced and led astray to mute idols. **3** Therefore I want you to know that no one who is speaking by the Spirit of God says, "Jesus be cursed," and no one can say, "Jesus is Lord," except by the Holy Spirit.

4 There are different kinds of gifts, but the same Spirit distributes them. **5** There are different kinds of service, but the same Lord. **6** There are different kinds of working, but in all of them and in everyone it is the same God at work.

7 Now to each one the manifestation of the Spirit is given for the common good. **8** To one there is given through the Spirit a message of wisdom, to another a message of knowledge by means of the same Spirit, **9** to another faith by the same Spirit, to another gifts of healing by that one Spirit, **10** to another miraculous powers, to another prophecy, to another distinguishing between spirits, to another speaking in different kinds of tongues,[a] and to still another the interpretation of tongues.[b] **11** All these are the work of one and the same Spirit, and he distributes them to each one, just as he determines.

Acts 3 - Peter Heals a Lame Beggar – One day Peter and John were going up to the temple at the time of prayer—at three in the afternoon. **2** Now a man who was lame from birth was being carried to the temple gate called Beautiful, where he was put every day to beg from those going into the temple courts. **3** When he saw Peter and John about to enter, he asked them for money. **4** Peter looked straight at him, as did John. Then Peter said, "Look at us!" **5** So the man gave them his attention, expecting to get something from them.

6 Then Peter said, "Silver or gold I do not have, but what I do have I give you. In the name of Jesus Christ of Nazareth, walk." **7** Taking him by the right hand, he helped him up, and instantly the man's feet and ankles became strong. 8 He jumped to his feet and began to walk. Then he went with them into the temple courts, walking and jumping, and praising God. **9** When all the people saw him walking and praising God, **10** they recognized him as the same man who used to sit begging at the temple gate called Beautiful, and they were filled with wonder and amazement at what had happened to him.

God was not just concerned with the suffering of our bodies but with the salvation of our souls. As a result of the fall of mankind, they became ill, disabled, in pain, and had all other forms of physical suffering. God is very sympathetic towards those who suffer physically and has a special grace towards these individuals, and we see evidence of this in the above quotes. The souls were redeemed and liberated by the divinely powerful, compassionate, and loving grace of God through Jesus.

Energy healers are either mediums or instruments channeling or directing God's love and healing light to everything or every being in need, including yourself. The unconditional love of the energy healers towards the healing of yourself and others is the divine way and in line with the Laws of the Universe. The world is a much more beautiful place when you live from the perspective of compassion and unconditional love for others.

Now that you understand that we are living in an entangled holographic universe where the energy we put out matters, it makes you more cognizant of your actions, thoughts, and words. Continue to work on your beliefs and have a better grasp on your true authentic self's divine path and know that the loving energy of God, True Source, Creator of all that is, will guide you along the way.

5
HIGHER VIBRATION

Before the sun goes down, forgive.
- Hawaiian proverb

Everything is energy and everything is connected. If we looked at an item such as a fork and put it under a high-powered microscope, we would see that it is made up of vibrating atoms. If we did the same thing with our hands, we would see that they are also vibrating atoms. The same goes for everything ever created, it is all energy that connects to each other on a quantum level.

Thoughts and feelings are also energy and the way we think and feel not only affects our mood, but it influences the energy and reality around us. We create our own reality by the thoughts we think and the frequency that we vibrate at.

The difference between higher vibration vs. lower vibration

We all vibrate at our own frequency and the higher the vibration the better we feel! This extends to our physical, emotional, and mental health. When we vibrate at a higher frequency, our emotions are easily dealt with, we're full of life, our lives flow with wondrous ease, and we feel fantastic inside and out. Choosing to live at a higher vibration means that you are an example to others. You might not fit in with the same group of friends anymore or connect with the same colleagues when you choose the light of living at a higher vibration. People may not approve of your commitment to live this way, but you will be able to find people who support you and resonate with you at a higher vibration because they are operating in the light as well.

Best Emotions (high vibration):

- ❖ Love;
- ❖ Compassion;
- ❖ Gratitude;
- ❖ Appreciation;
- ❖ Joy;
- ❖ Hope;
- ❖ Amusement;
- ❖ Inspiration;
- ❖ Awe;
- ❖ Enthusiasm;
- ❖ Contentment; and
- ❖ Euphoria.

With everything there is an opposite. We would not know light without darkness, health without sickness, or happiness without sorrow.

When we have a low frequency, our problems seem intolerable. When we have a lower vibration (frequency) our problems seem heavier, and our energy seems slower. We may experience things like pain, depression, sadness, and overwhelm. When vibrating at a lower frequency, we feel that life is an uphill battle, and we struggle to accomplish anything let alone our goals. Life takes on a negative quality and feels like a downward spiral. Toxic relationships can create and add to low frequency. We must find and recognize the destructive thought patterns, emotions, and habits that perpetuate low vibration in our lives and change them so that we can vibrate at a higher frequency.

Fight or flight is a psychological response to a real or perceived threatening situation. Our ancient ancestors when faced with danger in their environment (Sabre-tooth tigers, venomous snakes, fire, and attacks from other tribes) would choose either to fight or flee (flight). The psychological and physiological response to stress and threats prepare the body to react. In modern times, even though there is no longer a threat of ancient predators, one still has a fight or flight response to internal and external stressors such as worrying about health, physical impairments, work related issues, challenges with family or colleagues, and even preparing public speeches or presentations, or recalling past traumas will evoke a fight or flight response depending on one's beliefs and previous experiences.

Physical signs that fight or flight has been activated include:

- ❖ Dilated pupils- Dilated pupils allow more light into the eyes and results in better vision of surroundings;
- ❖ Skin tone - Skin will pale or flush depending on the person. Blood flow is reduced from surface areas and redirected to muscles and the brain; and
- ❖ Rapid heart rate and shallow breathing - Both are increased to provide the body with energy and oxygen to fight or flight.

Toxic emotions can also trigger a fight or flight response and manifest themselves in anxiety and panic attacks, disordered eating, self-harm, addiction, and more. It's important to be aware of the toxic emotions so that one can reflect and recognize them in order to change them. The first step of change is always awareness.

Toxic Emotions (low vibration):

- ❖ Anger;
- ❖ Guilt;
- ❖ Jealousy;
- ❖ Greed;
- ❖ Shame;
- ❖ Blame;
- ❖ Anxiety;
- ❖ Dissatisfaction;
- ❖ Hatred;
- ❖ Apathy;
- ❖ Fear; and
- ❖ Rejection.

Pay close attention to whatever triggers reactions from you. Your triggers reveal spots where old pain is still buried.
– ChildrenofLight

The Ego (Shadow Self)

The Ego is a self creation that is based on our experiences and environment. Ego directly translates to 'I' in Latin. Sometimes when the Ego is out of balance, we look down on others to reinforce our sense of superiority. We can find ourselves saying things like, "I'm a much better parent than her because I..." or "I'm much smarter than him because of my education and background..." or "I have a much nicer wardrobe than her..." etc. When you find yourself using the word 'I, Me, or Mine,' stop and examine what is happening internally. Are you coming from a place of Ego or a place of compassion, empathy, and reflection? Our thoughts, behaviours, and motives recede into the background when we work on an interesting and engaging task, are in flow, and are comfortable in our surroundings and with the people in them; we aren't concerned with what we want, or who we are, and what we can get out of the situation or person. When we operate from the Ego, we are vibrating at a lower frequency and can be demanding, demeaning, and conceited.

The Role of Genetic Inheritance

DNA gives our cells the blueprint for our body from conception to death. Though we may be able to change our hair colour, eye colour, and physical appearance, our DNA cannot be altered. As our soul enters our family (adoptive parents or biological parents) we inherit some of their unconscious vows, beliefs, and programming. The DNA of our ancestors has transformed, survived, and has made a deep impact while evolving for thousands of years.

We are born or adopted unto parents for a reason, we have come directly into the family line to help heal aspects of what no longer works genetically or spiritually.

We know we cannot choose our parents or families, but what if we were specifically sent to that family by True Source because there was unfinished business. What if we were there to stop the cycle, change the belief system, and make things better for the next generation?

A young woman told a story of her childhood. Every day the ice cream truck drove around her neighbourhood, with bells ringing, music playing, and children chasing. Every day she begged her mother to give her money for ice cream. Her mother said that the father had all the money and to go ask her dad. The young woman grew up with the limiting belief that men held the money and power in the relationship and that they should pay for everything. She got married and had the same expectations for her husband. Soon after getting divorced, she sought therapy and found out that part of the genetic inheritance she received was from her mother and grandmother who were both stay at home mothers and never had jobs outside of the home. They held the belief that men were the breadwinners and the primary providers. The beliefs became part of the grandmother and mother's spiritual DNA and were passed on to the granddaughter/daughter.

The young woman experienced what was part of her ancestral spiritual genetic inheritance, not just a learned behaviour. She spent her whole life trying to resolve the unconscious imprint on her soul's memory.

Spiritual inheritance is a soul vow with another being. Our ancestors can make helpful or harmful agreements with spiritual entities that can be passed down for generations. Even just by letting the entity into their space, our ancestors can influence our beliefs and these beliefs can direct our paths forward or backward.

One or more of your ancestors hundreds of years ago may have experienced physical and mental abuse as a child that was very damaging to their soul. Maybe they prayed for help and struck an agreement with a protective entity that helped them not be afraid or experience any more pain; instead of growing up, thanking the entity, and releasing it, they kept the agreement and decided they needed it to continue in their life to continue to feel protected.

Because of this, they passed this vow down to the next generation which may have led their children and children's children to feel the constant need for protection, avoiding processing or avoiding feeling all together because the entity's job was to continue to protect them.

Our soul will always try to resolve the unresolved by repeating the experience until we learn from it. Even if the experience was not our own, but instead our ancestors, their unresolved spiritual DNA needs to be released so that we can truly align with our soul.

Change your thoughts and you
Change the world.
– Norman Vincent Peale

<u>What it means to live at a higher vibration</u>

Your vibration is constantly changing and is rarely in a steady state. Our vibrations can shift from moment to moment throughout the day depending on our mood, how we feel physically, and the people and energy we surround ourselves with. Living in a high vibration centers on how you feel. Every vibration comes from within even though external circumstances can throw us off course. Have you ever jumped out of bed and stubbed your toe first thing in the morning? Or have you ever walked into a room and something or someone feels off? We often refer to this as a 'vibe' or 'bad energy'. How you react to such things changes your vibration. You can quite literally choose to live at a higher vibration by focusing on love, happiness, gratitude, and appreciation. Higher vibrations are also associated with spending time in nature and being connected to the Earth, laughing, sunshine (there's a reason why vitamin D is called the happiness or sunshine vitamin), and beautiful music. The idea of higher vibrational living means to add things to our lives that are positive and lift our own personal vibrations or frequency.

How to raise your vibration:

- ❖ Become conscious of your thoughts. Everything you think, say, and feel becomes your reality;
- ❖ Practice gratitude. Find something beautiful and appreciate it; speak sincere words of thanks to the universe and to those you come in contact with each day;
- ❖ Meditate. Spend time in nature and quiet your mind. Allow your intuition and higher self to guide you. Be still and breathe deeply;
- ❖ Love. Let someone know that you love them. Love yourself. Love your fellow humans;
- ❖ Generosity. Practice acts of kindness, care for one another, and give your gifts where you are able;
- ❖ Forgiveness. Forgive those that have hurt you. Forgive yourself. You deserve peace; and
- ❖ Spread your light. Pray for others, lift them up, let them know that you are thinking of them and sending them positive energy.

Be the light in the darkness.
The present moment is filled
With joy and happiness. If you are
Attentive, you will see it.
– Thich Nhat Hanh

Brain vs. Heart

Should we follow our heart or our brain? This is a question that plagues most of us at one point in time or another. When faced with challenges about life-changing decisions such as starting a new job, or moving our family across the country, or getting a divorce etc., our hearts and heads can give us conflicting opinions. Following our hearts over our heads can be a difficult task, but it is a rewarding one.

Following our heart means listening to our inner voice or intuition. When we listen to our inner voice or intuition, we can be inspired to be bold, take risks and chances that we otherwise may never take if we had listened to our brain. Our heart always wants us to say, *'why not'* rather than *'what if'*. Resisting our hearts can lead to many regrets such as being unable to tell someone how you feel and how much you love them, missed chances, and failed relationships. Following our hearts can lead us to finding and following our purpose and passions, making new connections, and changing the world.

When we listen to our hearts, we are vibrating at a high frequency, and this will allow more opportunities for fulfillment into our lives.

How are you vibrating right now? If you find that you are vibrating at a lower frequency, you now have the tools to correct that and raise your vibration.

Notes:

The struggle you're in today
Is developing the strength you
Need for tomorrow. – unknown

Limitations live only in our minds.
But if we use our imaginations,
Our possibilities become limitless. –
pixelstock.net

_____

_____

_____

_____

_____

_____

_____

_____

_____

_____

_____

_____

_____

_____

_____

_____

_____

_____

_____

_____

_____

Create with the heart; build with the mind.
— Criss Jamishs

_____

_____

_____

_____

_____

_____

_____

_____

_____

_____

_____

_____

_____

_____

_____

_____

_____

_____

_____

_____

_____

_____

_____

_____

If you feel like you don't fit in
This world, it is because you are
Here to help create a new one.
- unknown

_____
_____
_____
_____
_____
_____
_____
_____
_____
_____
_____
_____
_____
_____
_____
_____
_____
_____
_____
_____
_____
_____
_____

6

WESTERN VS. EASTERN MEDICINE
AND
THE PLACEBO EFFECT

The experience of pleasant, unpleasant, or neutral is the consequence of perception.
— Allan Lokos

Western and Eastern Medicine offer unique perspectives when it comes to fundamental healthcare. They are quite different in their approach in how they look at the human body and how each one treats and prevents illness. The Placebo effect is also explored and examined by both Western and Eastern practitioners with different beliefs and explanations.

Western Medicine

Conventional beliefs view the body as separate parts and pieces that are individualized, and Western medicine focuses on illness rather than reaching optimal levels of health. Western medicine only treats people after they are already sick and does not take into consideration the mind, body, and soul connection within. Breathing, meditation, and relaxation techniques are not taught in Western medicine and not widely understood by health care practitioners. The conventional medical system that we are used to is based on treating the symptom rather than the cause by using drugs, surgery, and anything else external. Conventional medicine does not recognize that thoughts and emotions are linked to overall health; learning to recognize thoughts that are harmful, destructive, or hurtful and replacing them with loving energy can quite literally save lives. (It is important to note that if you choose an alternative approach to healing, it is recommended to find a balanced approach using both Western medicine and alternative energy work.)

Western Medicine and the brain

The brain is viewed by conventional practitioners as a computer for the body. It controls the internal processes while a person is asleep (unconscious) or awake (conscious). Muscle contraction and movement decisions are made by the thalamus, basal ganglia, and the midbrain. The brain decides and initiates outgoing nerve impulses and determines overall behaviour.

When being treated by Western medicine practitioners, the medicine they prescribe is to treat a symptom or illness. The expectation is that this medicine works the same for each patient and this isn't always the case. Some people do not respond to the treatment and some people respond in unexpected ways. There is a chemical reaction when the prescribed medicine is introduced to the body and there also seems to be a neurobiological reaction as well in the brain due to expected results of the medication being administered. If you have a false expectation for the medication and what you falsely understood actually happens, this is a form of the placebo effect.

You are today where your thoughts have brought you,
And tomorrow you will be where your thoughts will bring you.
- James Allen

What is the Placebo Effect?

Think back to childhood. Did you experience a time when you scraped your knee, and a parent or loved one gave it a kiss and your pain disappeared? For those of you who can relate to that phenomenon, you're not alone. Western medicine often claims that energy healing is a pseudoscience and merely has a placebo effect on patients who were treated with energy healing in place of surgery or medication.

A placebo is a substance or treatment which is designed to have no therapeutic value. It's when an improvement of symptoms is observed despite using a non-active treatment. Research has found that the Placebo Effect can be helpful in easing things such as fatigue, depression, and pain. Pain and distress are rooted in complex brain functions. Taking a placebo can have measurable effects on healing the brain and body.

I would rather know the person who has the disease,
rather than the disease the person has.
— Hippocrates

Placebo treatments have been shown to cause the brain to release increased opioids and dopamine to release pain. When a placebo is given, dopamine receptors are engaged in sections of the brain that recognize rewards. How and why placebos work is still not fully understood by the scientific community.

Eastern Medicine

Eastern medicine (Traditional Chinese Medicine (TCM)) has evolved over thousands of years and TCM practitioners use multiple approaches to wellness such as Ayurveda, acupuncture, tai chi, and herbal medicines. The body is viewed holistically because in TCM it is believed that everything that makes up our body is interconnected, and each part has the ability to influence all other parts. The goal is to treat the whole body so that it maintains a balanced energy resulting in a vibrant and unburdened state of well-being.

Eastern medicine is not widely accepted in the parts of the world where Western or modern medicine are prevalent. There is a perception of mysticism surrounding Eastern medicine and, as a result, people say that the response to Eastern medicine practices is a placebo effect and that the results were made up in the client's mind and not as a result of the methods applied for the healing. It is possible that the neurobiological reaction related to the placebo effect is something that needs further investigation. The placebo effect is much more than what scientists currently believe it to be.

Energy healing has also been labeled having a placebo effect. People have been cured of cancer and many other illnesses during various forms of energy healing. When people say there is a placebo effect, they are usually implying the illness wasn't really there. In the case of cancer patients, the cancer was confirmed and very real. There is no denying this. By the cancer being removed during the energy healing methods you could say that the outcome is considered unexpected and, therefore, a placebo effect.

The placebo effect is one of the least understood phenomena in modern science, yet it is something that prevails time and time again. It is literal proof that humans have the ability to heal and create outcomes solely based on belief and expectations. If that is true, imagine how much more we are capable of if we learned how to tap into this way of being on a regular basis.
- *@anewme_a.w.*

Your ability to heal yourself is something that has been suppressed for centuries and it's time that we take back this knowledge and bring it front and center. Imagine how healthy we humans could be if we knew the real secret to life. We would be happy, healthy, full of love, and abundant. Disease will be a thing of the past.

Imagine the best case scenario for all situations.
Your mind will start to attract solutions.
- *@healingfacts*

7
BRAINWAVE STATES

Quiet the mind and the
Soul will speak.
– Ma Jaya Sati Bhagavati

Brainwaves are defined as oscillating electrical voltages in the brain measuring millionths of a volt. There are five fundamental brainwave states and unique things happen during each one.

Your brain changes brainwave states as you go from awake to sleep to deep sleep. Each state has a distinct function and benefits. During the day you might use both your Beta and Gamma waves and if you are fast asleep in the mid-REM cycle, you will be at higher levels of Delta and Theta waves. During your deepest REM sleep, your brain will be in the Gamma wave state. A healthy balance of each brainwave state daily will allow us to have a healthy state of mind.

Brainwave states

Beta

Beta brainwaves (12 – 40 Hz) are the higher frequency waves and are found during the normal waking state where you are fully awake and alert. Beta waves have a stimulating or arousing effect and too much of this brainwave could lead to stress, anxiety, and lack of attention. The right amount of Theta brainwaves will allow you to have consistent focus, strong memory recollection, and high problem-solving ability.

Alpha

Alpha brainwaves (8 – 12 Hz) are known as the "frequency bridge" between our conscious thinking (Beta) and our subconscious (Theta) Mind. When Alpha waves are present, you are calmer and have a deeper sense of relaxation and contentment.

Theta

Theta brainwaves (4 – 8 Hz) are known as "suggestible waves" due to them being the state your brain is in when you are in a trance or hypnotized. You are more susceptible to hypnosis and therapy during this state. These Theta waves are usually found when we are daydreaming or during restorative sleep where we have a more open and relaxed mind. With the right amount of Theta brainwaves, you will see the benefits of improved creativity, feeling whole, have a deeper emotional connection with yourself and others, being more intuitive, and feeling relaxed.

Delta

Delta brainwaves (0 – 4 Hz) are the slowest recorded brainwaves in humans and are related to many of our bodily functions such as regulating the cardiovascular and digestive systems. When you have enough Delta brainwaves during your sleep, you will wake up rested and refreshed and if you don't have enough Delta brainwaves then you may have learning difficulties or difficulties maintaining awareness.

Gamma

Gamma brainwaves (40 – 100 Hz) are used when you are processing more complex tasks and in general, for a healthy cognitive function. These waves are important for learning, memory and processing new information. Too much exposure to Gamma waves can lead to anxiety and stress and too little exposure could lead to depression, learning issues and even ADHD. When meditating and you reach the Gamma state, you feel a heightened state of completeness.

It is the theta state that we want to focus on because, in this state, you are able to communicate with your guides and/or your higher self. In this theta state, you have the potential to access extrasensory perception (ESP), experience remote viewing, connect with plants and plant matter, heal animals, heal other humans, and even the possibility of psychometry or perceive info from an object. You may obtain this theta state by practicing a modality of energy healing, lucid dreaming, or by meditation.

Meditation is the ultimate mobile device; you can use it anywhere, anytime, unobtrusively.
— Sharon Salzberg

Meditation

If you are looking to quiet your mind and learn how to remove negative thoughts and feelings from your daily life, then meditation could help you with this. It is a mental exercise that helps you to train yourself to focus on your attention and awareness. Some people meditate to relax. In a relaxed state, your brain waves (frequency) are around 8 – 12 Hz and this is called the alpha state. In deeper meditations the brain waves go to 4 – 7 Hz, or the theta state.

The benefits of meditation

With practice, you will be able to calm your mind which improves your focus resulting in being more productive. With as little as 10 minutes a day you can increase your brain's alpha waves that are associated with relaxation which may cause a decrease in stress, anxiety, and depression. Deeper healing occurs at the theta state as well as the potential to communicate with your higher self or your guides.

Just feel the magic in the air and the power of the breeze,
Feel the energy of the plants, the bushes and the trees,
Let yourself be surrounded by nature at its best,
Calm yourself, focus and let magic do the rest.
- Sally Walker

Types of meditation

Mindfulness Meditation and Loving-Kindness are types of meditation. In Mindful Meditation you focus on either your breath, a word or mantra phrase. This method has been shown to decrease distraction and your analytical mind to help you let go of your thoughts and be in the moment. Loving-Kindness Meditation is where you are sending love and kindness to others. This can help boost your empathy and compassion that may help you avoid charged responses to negative thoughts. There are also active and passive meditations. In passive meditations you focus on clearing your thoughts and breathing, and active meditations are related to reconnecting your body, mind, and soul.

Lucid Dreaming

Lucid dreaming is a type of dream where the dreamer knows they are dreaming and can exert some control over what happens in their dream. This is a dream state where the dreamer is conscious, and it happens during the REM (Rapid Eye Movement) part of the sleep cycle. It feels very real and what you experience is often extremely vivid. Your five senses are heightened, and your emotions can feel very intense. In this world you create your own reality all while being in the safe construct of your own mind. The benefits of lucid dreaming are that you can take control of night terrors and realize that they are not real, live out fantasies, access your beliefs that are in your subconscious and work on them allowing you to conquer your biggest fears, learn or practice new skills, manifest your best you, increased motor skills, reduce nightmares, relieve anxiety, enhanced creativity, and travel anywhere in the world and beyond. The drawbacks are that lucid dreaming may cause dreamers to become confused between reality and fantasy.

Follow your dreams
They know the way.
– askideas.com

How to lucid dream

One way to become aware if you are dreaming is to ask yourself throughout the day if you are dreaming. With the repetition throughout the day, you will be more likely to ask yourself if you are dreaming while you are dreaming. You can test yourself as well by interacting with objects in your waking world by touching them. In the waking world you cannot push your hand through a wall but in the dream world you can. You cannot fly in the waking world but in the dream world you can. Look at your hands, mirrors, clocks, etc., and in the dream world these may look different. When you go to bed tell yourself that you will be awake in your dreams. At some point you will realize that you are dreaming and then the rest is up to you. Be creative.

When this first happened to me, I was so excited that I woke up. Everything comes with practice. Keep a journal on your bedside table and record your dreams. You may not realize it at first, but you receive messages from your higher self and your guides in your dreams and as you write your dreams down you will notice these messages. You may even have a conversation with your higher self while lucid dreaming. Anything is possible in the dream realm.

Your visions will become clear only when you can look into your own heart. Who looks outside, dreams; who looks inside, awakes.
– C. G. Jung

Keeping a dream journal beside your bed can aid you in remembering and interpreting your dreams. By increasing your awareness while you are awake, you can enhance your awareness during the dream state because your levels of consciousness are the same.

Reality testing trains the mind to recognize your awareness while you are awake. By doing reality checks throughout the day, you will be able to induce awareness while dreaming.

Reality checks can include:

- ❖ Mirrors- While dreaming, your reflection will look abnormal. Maybe it's an alteration of yourself such as a different hair colour, eye colour, or facial feature;
- ❖ Fingers- Try and push your fingers against the opposite hand. You are dreaming if they pass through;
- ❖ Reading- If you're dreaming about reading something, look

away from the text and then back again, it will change;
- ❖ Pinch- You'll be able to breathe if you pinch your nose while dreaming; and
- ❖ Tattoos/Piercings- If you have tattoos or piercings, they'll look different in a dream.

Pick one reality check to do several times a day so that you can train yourself to recognize your awareness in your dreams.

Techniques

It is possible to initiate lucid dreaming even though it is random for the most part. Induction techniques can help:

- ❖ Mnemonic induction of lucid dreams (MILD). Tell yourself that you will have a lucid dream tonight. Do it before bed or when you're awake during Wake Back To Bed.
- ❖ Wake back to bed (WBTB). Wake up five hours after bedtime and when you go back to sleep, you'll likely enter REM sleep while you're still conscious.
- ❖ Wake-initiated lucid dream (WILD). During wake-initiated lucid dreaming you enter REM sleep from wakefulness while maintaining your consciousness.

Using these techniques with reality testing and dream journaling can increase your chances of lucid dreaming.

Dreams are today's answers
To tomorrow's questions.
– hative.com

There are eight different types of dreams:

- ❖ Daydreams - Studies show that adults daydream on average for 70-120 minutes per day. Daydreams are a level of consciousness between being asleep and awake and occur during our waking hours when we let our imaginations wander.

❖ Lucid dreams - Where the dreamer is aware they are dreaming. Lucid dreamers have cultivated the skills of active participation in their dreams.

❖ Nightmares - Can be a subconscious response to real life trauma and difficult situations in the dreamer's waking life. Nightmares can also be an indication of something that needs to be acknowledged and confronted in reality.

❖ Recurring dreams - Happen when there is a situation in reality that has not been resolved. A repeated conflict that remains unsolved or ignored will show itself in recurring dreams.

❖ Healing dreams - Messages for the dreamer regarding their health. Our bodies are able to communicate to us through dreams and can be telling us that we need to visit a health practitioner or healer.

❖ Prophetic dreams - Also known as psychic dreams. These dreams can help us tell the future. Our unconscious mind knows what is coming before our conscious mind can piece together overlooked information.

❖ Signal dreams - This type of dream helps us make decisions in our waking lives. For example, if the dreamer dreams of skydiving, it could be a signal to take a risk, go all in, take a chance, and trust the outcome.

❖ Epic dreams - Are compelling, vivid, and impossible to ignore. The intricate details of this type of dream stay with the dreamer for years and make the dreamer feel as if they have had a life-changing experience.

During meditations you may achieve the alpha and theta brainwave states and enjoy the benefits of reduced stress or anxiety, and the potential benefit of healing. In lucid dreaming you are in the theta brainwave state where you are able to control and explore your dream on a whole new level. During these states you have the opportunity to work on yourself and clear out some of the clutter holding you back from being your true authentic self. In addition to having the ability to heal yourself, the theta brainwave state is also where you have the potential to talk to your higher self or your guides. If you need answers or guidance, the theta brainwave state creates a bridge for you to access this information.

Communication with your higher self or guides

Everyone has the ability to communicate with their guides. Clearing out the clutter and calming your mind is key for you to begin the learning process. A quiet mind is best to be able to see, hear, sense, etc., your higher self or guides. You will need to practice to grow your skill and 10 - 20 minutes a day is plenty. Most of you will learn to connect with your higher self or guides through meditation and some may be able to connect during lucid dreaming. You even receive messages in your non-lucid dreams, and you can keep a journal on your bedside table for tracking them. There are sometimes obvious messages in your dreams and most of the time it is a bit cryptic, and you'll need to analyze them. As you track your dreams and learn how to analyze them you will notice patterns and the messages intended for you are easier to see. For meditations, you will need to learn how to get into the deep meditation theta brainwave state and with practice this will become second nature. There are guided meditations that you can listen to on YouTube to practice and I have some meditations in The Healing Journey chapter as well. Practice regularly and grow your abilities.

How you communicate with your higher self and guides

You use your intuition to speak with your higher self and

guides. This is achieved by using one or a few of your eight intuitive senses.

Clairvoyance

Clairvoyance is where you clearly see with your mind's eye. You have what people call visions or you see symbols. You usually find people with this ability who are psychics, fortune tellers, etc. When your third eye or ajna chakra is open, it is easier to be clairvoyant.

Clairsentience

Clairsentience is where you have a clear feeling in your physical body and is where the phrase "gut instinct" comes from. You can feel in your gut that something is off with a circumstance.

Claircognizance

Claircognizance is clear knowing. Sometimes you find that you know something without knowing how you know. Information just pops into your head, and you know that it is correct. You are essentially tapping into the Source Field and are receiving downloads of knowledge.

Clairaudience

Clairaudience is clear audio/hearing, and this happens when you hear sounds from the etheric realm. What you hear is usually unexpected and sometimes unexplainable. When your ears ring or click it is a sign that you are receiving information.

Clairsalience

Clairsalience is clear smelling and is when you smell something that cannot be explained like cigarette smoke and there is no one near you smoking. You may smell things that are related to past events.

Clairgustance

Clairgustance is clear tasting where you spontaneously taste something that is not in your mouth. Many chefs have this ability, and it allows them to intuitively put flavours together for the perfect recipe. It also occurs when your body is craving something for nourishment.

Clairtangency

Clairtangency is clear touching, and you use this to get information from touching an object. Some psychics hold a possession of yours like a ring to see information about your past, present, or future. Energy healers also use this method to determine where your energy is blocked.

Clairempathy

Clairempathy is clear emoting and is common for most people. This is where you sense the emotions of others and without creating proper energetic boundaries you might absorb those energies which will cause you to feel drained.

Listen to the universe.
It is always whispering you messages through songs,
dreams, numbers, animals, and thoughts.
– unknown

I track my dreams and visions in a journal and would like to share some of them with you. They are the ones that really stand out and brought about me writing this book.

I am a daydreamer
And a night thinker.
– intelligence

Dreams and Visions related to this book

Visions

I saw a big beautiful barn owl flying directly at me and after doing research found that "seeing" a barn owl means that you are receiving enlightenment at that time. Something hidden is being revealed. Around this time I was opening up to new ways of learning about energy healing and thought about writing this book.

During a grounding meditation I saw a rhino at the end. Rhinos symbolize an intimate connection to the Earth. This makes the rhino a perfect symbol for confidence, assurance, steadiness, and sure footedness. For me, it represents that I am very grounded and connected to the earth's energies and have let go of the negative energies that are no longer useful or helpful for me. This vision is brought to you in this book, helping you to embrace the strength and spirit of the rhino and go forward with confidence knowing that your healing journey is beginning and with each day you will see more and more how wonderful you are. As you change your perspective you will discover your true authentic self and I guarantee that you will be very happy with what you discover.

Dreams

I was in a stadium and after giving a presentation I saw a man on the big screen at the far end of the stadium and in my earpiece, I could hear him tell me that my limo is waiting up ahead, my name is Lynn Theta, and the driver will be holding a sign with my name on it. After doing some research, Theta is a

Divine word, and the Milky Way galaxy is in the shape of the Theta symbol (the math geek in me likes this). Theta also represents an "Escort/Messenger" and "Divine Essence outflow Meta/Medium". I believe it is my Divine Purpose to be a messenger and help as many people as possible to find their true authentic self and understand that we all have the power to heal ourselves. Suffering is manmade and we have gifts that, once we are aware of them, will remove all suffering from us.

I was undergoing a metamorphosis of some kind - my mouth felt like it was full of stringy roots and seeds – almost like I was turning into a plant or tree from the inside out. It was a very loving and interconnected sense of community and as I continued my research of other healing modalities, I became more aware of my connection with EVERYTHING. This interconnected physical root system is the same as the interconnected Energy System of the Universe. It is a beautiful feeling when you realize how you are connected on a quantum level to everything and that your loving energy causes a ripple effect that spans the Universe. I hope this book may help you find this connection.

I heard a voice say, "The people need to be happier". It was an inspiration for me to write this book so I can help people figure out how to break out of the darkness and find happiness, peace, love, and abundance.

I had a cluster of dreams that all had the same theme. It was people living their multiple lives on different paths, but they all end the same. No matter which path you're on, you will use your free will to evolve and become your true authentic self. Some paths are longer than others, but you ultimately end up where you are meant to be. We all have our own path to follow. We come into the world with experiences that we must go through. In doing so we address the issues that have held us back from evolving in our past lives. If we realize that we are in a negative loop (eg., repeated bad relationships), then we can make changes and break out of that loop. This is a process in the evolution of your soul. With each challenge overcome, you get one step closer to your true authentic self.

Now that you understand the varying frequencies of brainwave states you are better equipped with the knowledge to have the best experiences while meditating, lucid dreaming, and communicating with your higher self or guides. Enjoy exploring this new world.

Dream Journal:

Dreams are illustrations...
From the book your soul
Is writing about you
— Marsha Norman

Only as high as I reach can I grow,
Only as far as I seek can I go,
Only as deep as I look can I see,
Only as much as I dream can I be.
— funpulp.com

Follow your dreams.
Let your heart believe
Feel your spirit soar
Imagine what can be.
— QuotesGram

_____

_____

_____

_____

_____

_____

_____

_____

_____

_____

_____

_____

_____

_____

_____

_____

_____

_____

_____

_____

_____

If you can dream it
You can do it.
— hdnicewallpapers.com

8
COMMON APPROACH FOR HEALING

Clear your energetic field.
Ground into your body and into the earth.
Create a protective shield.
Connect in with your guidance from your cosmic self.
– unknown

Using energy to heal is not a new concept and was first understood thousands of years ago by Chinese healers (Eastern medicine); twelve pathways of energy in the body interweave limbs and organs together in a complex network. When the energy field is powerful and flourishing, the person remains balanced and healthy. When the energy field is weakened by things like guilt, jealousy, stress, anger, sorrow, and grief, the body becomes weary, sick, and eventually dies. Everything we need to heal comes from within. This concept of healing from the inside out has been available to us since the beginning of time.

Basic methods of healing such as alternative medicines, healing modalities, and relaxation techniques are very valuable and much needed in our high-tech lives. Each human has ancient wisdom inside of them. We have a natural intelligence with an electromagnetic pull guiding us toward health. Anything that takes us away from this natural intelligence and healing creates disease. Energy healers can positively work with the energy field of the body to influence health. Various techniques such as meditation, chanting, reflexology, reiki, and other modalities have helped patients recover from various illnesses and maintain good health.

It is only by grounding our
Awareness in the living sensation
Of our bodies that the "I AM",
Or our real presence, can awaken.
– George Ivanovich Gurdjieff

<u>What is energy healing?</u>

All matter, everything in the universe, including our physical bodies, is made up of vibrations of energy. Magnets, crystals, and our own hands can make energy move, and by changing the energy field, stagnation and sickness can be removed and replaced with loving and healing energy. The flow of energy through the body and how it flows directly relates to health. Drugs and surgery should be a last resort while non-invasive methods that integrate the mind, body, and soul should be first steps in healing; many modalities can be performed alone or with an energy healer in the comfort of your home. Alternative medicine practitioners focus on healing the source or root of the disease, illness, and sickness while conventional practitioners focus on suppressing symptoms. A genuine intention to heal with positive loving thoughts is known as quantum thinking and it invokes healing that takes place at a spiritual level. The inner voice should not be discounted as the way one speaks internally can be damaging and disease inviting or uplifting and healing to your body. Limiting and inherited beliefs can also affect the subconscious and cause sickness, discord, and harm within the body. Energy healing can offer release of this destructive way of thinking. Everything begins and ends in the mind and there cannot be a world (internal or external) without the mind first entering into it. As above (the mind/energy) so below (the physical body).

Until you make the unconscious conscious,
it will direct your life and you will call it fate.
- Carl G Jung

The conscious, subconscious, and unconscious mind and collective consciousness

The conscious mind defines all thoughts and actions in our awareness. For example, the enjoyment of a beautiful bouquet of flowers, the pain of a stubbed toe, or the annoyance of a traffic jam. Our awareness of self and the world around us is consciousness. Consciousness means quite literally, awake.

The subconscious mind defines all reactions as automatic actions that we become aware of when we think about them. An example would be driving to work and not realizing how we got there until we pull into the parking lot. One's actions and feelings are driven by influences of the mind in which one is not fully aware.

The unconscious mind defines all past events and memories and is where your beliefs reside; it is a reservoir of feelings, thoughts, and urges that are outside of the conscious awareness. Sometimes, no matter how hard we try, we cannot recall a memory such as what it felt like to take our first steps, or the first time we tried strained peas as a baby.

Collective consciousness is defined as a set of shared beliefs, ideas, and moral attitudes which operate as a unifying force within society. Collective consciousness refers to a shared understanding of social norms in a set of ideologies that bind people together. Perhaps you've experienced collective consciousness at a religious function where people have been chanting in unison, or while at a mass meditation event.

Wouldn't it be great to be part of a collective consciousness where everyone is vibrating at 4th or 5th density levels? What an awesome experience that would be!

Life is a school where you
Learn how to remember
What your soul already knows.
- unknown

Common Healing Structure

Although there are many healing modalities, there is a common structure throughout them all. They encourage the integration of the mind, body and soul. Breathing, meditation, energy, intention, and guided imagery are among some of the tools that encourage healing as well as an awareness of self and an element of self-discovery. These practices work to bring balance to the entire body, mind, and soul. Holistic fusion among all the energies of the body, mind, and soul allows you to find peace and abundance in your daily life.

Practicing one or more of the healing modalities will enable you to find a balance between your mind, body, and soul. As you calm your mind, find a neutral space in your heart, clear your chakras from beliefs that are neither helpful nor useful, and learn to be in a constant state of gratitude, you will find that you are able to heal your past traumas and vibrate at a higher frequency.

You will begin to enjoy a happy, loving, and abundant life.

I lovingly release the past
And turn my attention to this new day.
All is well.
– Louise Hay

Common Steps for healing:

Please note that these steps are in sequence. Each step builds into the next step. Steps 1-6 are your basic steps to prepare for steps 7-10. Once you connect with your chakras, step 7, they will remain open, so this step only needs to be done once.

The common steps for healing are:

1) Find your awareness;
2) Ground yourself;
3) Clear your mind;
4) Quiet your mind;
5) Find your energy connection;
6) Create your boundaries;
7) Connect with your chakras;
8) Open and clear your heart;
9) Clear your chakras;
10) Clear your past traumas; and
11) Be grateful.

General Routine for the steps

Daily

Practicing steps 1-6 and 1-5 & 11 daily will allow you to start your day with clear thoughts, a positive perspective, and your boundaries in place to protect you from negative energy you may encounter during your day. The best way to end your day is with gratitude. Focus only on what you are grateful for and let the rest fall away. You will find that you sleep better and wake up refreshed when you have a grateful and loving heart.

2-3 times per week or as needed

Practicing steps 1-6 & 8 two to three times per week will help to open and clear your heart of negative energy. This will help you to be more compassionate and loving and maintain a higher vibrational energy.

Once per week or as needed

Practicing steps 1-6 & 9 once per week will allow you to keep your chakras clear of negative energy or unhelpful beliefs. This will help you to have a healthy vibration and a positive outlook and you may feel an improvement in your happiness and overall wellbeing.

Clearing your past traumas

Practice steps 1-6 & 10. This you do on a timeline that works best for you. You could work on this daily, every other day, three days per week or once per week. This is totally up to you and what you can manage. It is a very emotional process to release all of that hurt and there is no wrong way to go about it. It is all about you and your healing journey. Find your own pace and the most important part is do not put this off. It is time to get your life back so start today. It is worth it. You will be so happy to be free from the burden of those negative energies.

The common steps explained:

1) Find your awareness – This is where you learn the difference between your physical self and energetic self. In your physical world you can see, smell, taste, touch, and hear.

These are tangible things that you are familiar with. You also have an energetic self that we explored in brainwave states where your body vibrates and emits energy. In the effects of conscious intention on human DNA you find that your intentions have energy and have a physical impact in our world. Your awareness is when you find the balance between your physical and energetic self. When you are thinking, you are using your brain and when you are aware of where you are thinking you are identifying that place in your energetic body. You find that when you are thinking your awareness is in your head, usually behind your eyes and between your ears. Take time to practice finding your awareness and moving it around your body. Move it side to side between your ears, down your leg and into your foot, and out your arm and into your hand. When you master this try sending your awareness outside your body. You'll be fascinated by the results. Finding your awareness allows you to be more connected with yourself and when you are more connected with yourself you are able to heal yourself.

2)   Ground yourself to the Earth Energy. Feel a connection from the root chakra, at the base of your spine, to the Earth's core. Physically, we are connected or grounded to the earth by gravity, and we need to ground our soul energy as well. This is done using your imagination and awareness. When doing any kind of energy work, it is important to ground your energy first. Imagine an energetic cord connecting your base chakra to the Earth's core. This keeps you grounded. As you practice grounding yourself you will begin to notice when you are not grounded. You will feel negative energies affecting you and these negative energies could be someone in your energy space, being distracted by unnecessary details, an irrational fear, being clumsy, or a general feeling of things being off. Grounding yourself will help you to have grounded energy levels which allow for a nice flow of your energy throughout your day. I love grounding my bedroom and I find I sleep better knowing that it is grounded. I gently declare the space my space and I also set the intention for loving

energies to be there throughout the night.

3)   Clear your mind – Your mind is a place where you should be able to feel at peace and can think. Sometimes when I try to think I find that there is a lot of clutter or noise from outside influences preventing me from being able to focus and use my brain effectively. Outside distractions or influences taking up your brain power must be released. One of the main reasons you have difficulty connecting with your inner self and energy is due to noise. This noise can be from a physical source or from an energetic source. Physical sources can be avoided but energetic sources are internal and cannot be avoided. The most common energetic source of noise is overthinking. A racing scattered mind is very unproductive. Even things like unimportant details can get your mind going in circles. Overthinking causes stress, leads to your ego or shadow self taking over, and it is difficult to make important decisions. Clearing your mind of all noise is very important so that you can stop focusing on those unnecessary details or beliefs that hold you back from doing what you are meant to do and being your true authentic self.

4)   Quiet your mind. I am hyper analytical, and this is a big one for me. This is where you turn down the overactive part of your brain. To turn down the noise in your mind you can use your imagination. Find a way that works best for you to turn down the noise. I visualize blinds or curtains in my mind. I close them and this blocks out the noise for me. Experiment with different approaches to quiet your mind. The impact this will have on you is amazing and I can't wait for you to be free of the noise that is holding you back.

5) Find your energetic connection – You are energy, and you are surrounded by energy. Connecting with the energy outside your physical body is already happening and while using your awareness you will be able to feel this connection more clearly. Earth energy enters your body through your feet and all the other

energy enters through your crown chakra. Earth energy typically goes in your feet, up your legs, through your base chakra and returns to the earth by going down the other leg, through your feet back into the earth. This cycle of energy grounds you, energizes you, and clears your root chakra of any negative energy.

When you call in the Divine Source energy or True Source energy it enters through your crown chakra and goes down the back of your sushumna (the energy channel that the body chakras are connected to) to your base chakra and then travels up the front of the sushumna. When the energy gets to your shoulders some of it goes out your arms to your hands and then the energy leaves your hands through a chakra that is at the center of your palm.

The rest of the energy goes out your crown chakra and flows up and out like a fountain in all directions and as it goes downward it circles into the base chakra and continues flowing in this pattern as illustrated in the torus energy field. Try practicing putting your palms facing each other about the length of your hand apart. You should be able to feel the energy flowing. There may be some resistance or pressure or heat between your hands after 10 – 20 seconds.

If you don't feel it right away, keep practicing. Remember to follow all the steps above prior to doing any energy work. When you find your energy connection you can use your awareness to see where in your body you need to send this energy and then place it or send it there. Track your progress and see if you feel better. In Reiki you let the energy flow from the palms of your hands and place them where you want to be healed or, if you can't reach the area, lovingly intend the energy to go where you want it to go. Again, be sure all the above steps are in place prior to doing a healing.

6) Create boundaries – The outermost part of your torus field is where your Aura ends, and the outer energies begin. Your aura is flexible and can be close to your body or far away from your body. You use your awareness to sense where your aura is and to move it to varying distances from your body. It is important to protect yourself from external energies that you do not want to come into contact with. You don't want to have other people's energy crossing your boundary and affecting your energy.

Sometimes you may find yourself in an environment that is negative and having your boundary in check will help you have a better experience in that environment. If you close your eyes and use your imagination and awareness you will be able to sense your aura and where it is. Be centered in your aura and have it a comfortable space away from you. This will be your shield against negative energy. You need to put an intention into your space and the outside space. The space between the aura and yourself is your space. Be kind and declare this space only for yourself. Outside the aura is for everyone and everything else. Be kind and declare this space for everyone else. If you want to put something in your aura as a visual for the boundary you may. Use your imagination and find an object or just add texture to your aura in a way that works for you. I have a honeycomb grid in my aura, and this allows me to keep a healthy boundary when I am interacting with others and their energies.

Having boundaries is really important for everyone and those who are empaths need it even more. Ensure your boundaries are in place when you go out into public spaces so that you don't absorb all of the unbalanced energies. Having boundaries protects you from absorbing the energies of others. When you have this mastered, no one will be able to affect your energy without your consent. When you respect yourself and your boundaries, your daily interactions and life will flow much better, and you will feel more at peace in what were once uncomfortable surroundings.

7) Connect with your chakras. There are meditations on YouTube that attune/activate your chakras. You may also ask Divine Source during a meditation for attunements so that you can connect with your Chakras and be sure to receive this blessing with gratitude. Once you have your chakras attuned, you can use your imagination, awareness, and the image used for the Chakras to energetically find their placement. Take your awareness from your mind and visit your chakras. Practice this until you are comfortable at "feeling", "sensing", or "seeing" your chakras. While using your awareness you will be able to sense if there are any dark areas in your chakras that need clearing.

8) Open and clear your heart (non-physical heart where you feel emotions also known as the inner heart) from all negative energy. This is a continuous work as you heal past traumas and negativity in your life. When you take your awareness to your heart and see some shadows, you can send an intention that you no longer need that energy, release it and let it go to the earth to be grounded and cleansed. There are meditations for opening and clearing your heart. My favourite meditation is the Open Heart Meditation by *Natural Way of Living. (*Please note that I am in no way promoting this organization, or any other, mentioned in this book. I am merely stating that this is my favourite open heart meditation and it helped me heal my past traumas.)

9) Clear your chakras. (This is also known as clearing your beliefs or doing shadow work). When you use your awareness to look into your chakras and see the dark spots, these are the beliefs that you have created during your experiences so far in your life. Many if not all of these beliefs need to be cleared as they are inaccurate and neither useful nor helpful. Using your imagination and awareness, find these places in your chakras, taking one chakra at a time, releasing what no longer serves you to the earth to be grounded and cleansed. I use an earth grounding vacuum to clear out my beliefs. Now that I see this on paper it looks a little funny, but it is the best visual for me and is

very effective. As you clear out negative energy you need to replace it with neutral loving and healing energy from Divine Source; call in the loving neutral energy to fill the spaces where you released energy. Continue this replenishing until you feel whole and at peace. The opposite can also be done – add new beliefs to your chakras. Bring them in through your crown chakra. I am worthy, I am loved, I am enough, etc... As you connect with and clear your Chakras you will feel your energy transform. With each level opened and cleared, you will feel lighter, and you will feel the pure light or energy that you are made of. You will also feel more connected to all that is in this entangled holographic universe.

10) Clear your past traumas. This step may take some time. Be patient. Be kind and love yourself unconditionally. In Reiki you learn that there is no time or distance in the energy realm, and this allows you to go back in time to heal traumas. This was the part of my learning journey that had the most impact on my life. Learning how to heal past traumas freed me in a way that is difficult to describe. No longer having an emotional attachment to the events that were devastating to me was a freedom that made my life change dramatically. One way to do this is to bring them up individually. You forgive the cause of the trauma, you forgive yourself for being traumatized, and then you send love to the cause of the trauma and yourself. This does not mean that what happened was ok but it helps you let go of the negative emotions related to the trauma so that it no longer affects you. Replace all the negative emotions with unconditional love and you will heal. Repeat until all your past traumas are healed. Healing with love (loving yourself unconditionally and sending unconditional love) is the most effective way as this is in alignment with the laws and the energy of the Divine Cosmos. Unconditional self-love, sending unconditional love, and forgiveness are the most important factors in healing your past traumas. I wholeheartedly recommend you do this. The lightness you will feel as the healing process progresses compares to nothing. It is the most liberating

experience in my opinion. You will break out of the darkness and finally find peace.

11) Be Grateful. Always be in a state of gratitude for all the above. In general, it is best to be in a state of gratitude as a daily practice. This alone will have an immensely positive impact on your life. Practice being grateful – Try journaling about experiences where you chose to be grateful rather than seeing the negative in a situation. Write how you felt as a result of choosing to be grateful.

Gratitude turns what we have into enough.
– Melody Beaettie

What are you grateful for in your life? Perhaps it's opening your eyes each morning or for your strength and energy that is emerging even in the face of challenges. When we focus on gratitude, stress melts away, we become one with the universe, and we can see things from a different perspective. When we feel out of balance, return to gratitude.

Gratitude is universal, yet it is something deeply personal and it can even come from observing difficult lessons learned. The grass is grateful for the sun, but also for the rain. We cannot observe perfect health without knowing what sickness is. We can be grateful for the observance of the opposite. Remove resistance by allowing your path of healing to appear and may gratitude fill your heart.

Gratitude:

Start each day with a grateful heart.

-7minds.com

_____

_____

_____

_____

_____

_____

_____

_____

_____

_____

_____

_____

_____

_____

_____

_____

_____

_____

_____

_____

_____

_____

_____

We can only be said to be
ALIVE
In those moments when our hearts
Are conscious of our treasures.
- Localadventurer.com

Stop...
Notice...
Appreciate...
Welcome to now...
- blog.thewellnessuniverse.com

*Joy is really the simplest form
of gratitude.*

- Karl Barth

9
THE HEALING JOURNEY

A walk in nature walks
The soul back home.
− Mary Davis

When you begin your journey learning about the energetic realm you find out that distance and time do not exist there. This allows you to send healing energy to the past and positive energy to the future.

I took full advantage of the education I received regarding healing past traumas and experiences. With each course I began to heal my past. There were meditations you could do on your own and this allowed me to continue to work on loving my past self and letting go of all the experiences that shattered my soul.

This is not an easy task and starting is the most important step.

As you go into your past experiences you relive them. This causes the pain to come front and center and although it might be difficult to imagine reliving these experiences it is necessary. You need to feel that pain to heal the pain. In order for you to find peace you must forgive what caused you this pain, forgive yourself for being in pain, let go of the dark energy and replace it with love and light – send love to the cause and send love to yourself. Replace the darkness with love and light.

Three Stages of Healing:
1) Recognize you have outgrown some way of being and that is no longer serving you.
2) Doing the inner energy work to transform that part of your identity, beliefs and programs.
3) Embodying the lesson by becoming the new expanded version of you.
- Maryam Hasnaa

Many people have difficulty forgiving and I understand that strong emotion. Sadly, this causes illness in the individual who refuses to forgive. I know people who refuse to forgive, and their life is filled with physical pain, fear, jealousy, and paranoia. They also have very poor health and suffer mental illness. What is worse, forgiving and being free from the never-ending cycle of suffering and finally feeling at peace or continue the self-destructive dark energy pattern that you are currently in causing you to have poor health, bad relationships and/or feeling like you're drained of energy every single second of the day and not sleeping well at night?

Forgiving does not mean that you condone what caused you the pain. It is a means of letting go of the emotions attached to the experience. Sending love to the cause is what a pure heart is meant to do. Remove the attachment to the cause and be free of the emotions that cause you pain and suffering.

My process is healing during meditation. During the meditation, I practice steps 1 – 6, 8 & 10 of the Common Steps for Healing in Chapter 8, Common Approach for Healing. I find the Open-Heart Prayer (meditation) is an excellent guided meditation for my overall state of well-being. Part of this meditation allows me to forgive the cause of past experiences and forgive myself. It really is a beautiful meditation and is where I do most of my past trauma healing.

Once you learn the process for forgiving, sending unconditional love to the cause and yourself, letting go of energy that no longer serves you, you can do meditations to let go of unwanted energy or emotions attached to past traumas or experiences. Just 20-30 minutes a day is all you need. Give yourself permission to let go of the emotional energy that is no longer helpful or useful. This is not something that can be rushed because the energy has been held in your body for many years and sometimes lifetimes and will heal over time. For some, you will feel immediate release and for others it will take some time. Be patient and let your healing guide the process.

Love yourself. Be kind. You are on your healing journey. It's your turn to break out of the darkness.

> *I release the past with love.*
> *I choose to voice only love.*
> – Louise Hay

Grounding While Walking

We know that walking provides a whole host of benefits and when combined with intentional gratitude, the results of raising our vibration are clear. Some of the additional benefits of walking in gratitude include elevation of mood, raising your vibration, stress-release, filling ourselves up with loving and grounding energies, appreciation of things from a new perspective, and intuition guidance.

Before you begin your Walk of Gratitude, set an intention for yourself.

Some intentions can be:

❖ To find beauty all around me and thank the creator for it;

❖ To appreciate the things that I cannot control and be happy that I do not have to control others or circumstances;

❖ To be grateful for the differences of opinion and perspective of those in my life; or

❖ To be thankful for where I am currently in the universe and for where I am headed.

As you begin, feel your feet rooted in the ground and connect with nature and the Life Force energy. Breathe deeply and saturate the thirty trillion cells of your body with the feeling of unconditional love, gratitude, and high vibrations.

Walk as if you are kissing the Earth with your feet.
— Thich Nhat Hanh

A Walk of Gratitude:

As an example, for you to feel the energy that surrounds you, I recommend trying A Walk of Gratitude. Go outside and find a peaceful place that has lush vegetation, birds, etc. (be in nature), where you can try this practice. Clear and quiet your mind and with each step feel the loving intention from your inner-heart (the place where you feel emotions); First step – Thank you. Second step – I love you. Repeat. Be grateful for being grounded in nature and allow negativity to be released through your feet and cleansed by the very loving Earth Energy. After 15-20 minutes you should feel some release or maybe you will feel a little lighter. During this walk you will learn what unconditional love feels like which will help you understand how you will feel in a loving and compassionate life without expectations. It is important that your brain and thoughts remain quiet. When you work from the heart, the brain can sometimes get in the way. As you progress with your learning you will be able to find balance between the heart and the brain and this will result in a very beautiful experience during your walk of gratitude. With a calm, quiet mind, and grateful, open heart, it is also possible that you may receive some insights from your higher self during your walk of gratitude. Enjoy the unconditional love, healing, and guidance as you walk in gratitude.

<u>I Am Worthy (meditation):</u>

❖ Set your intention. Your intention is more important than any technique that you choose to use. By setting your intention on loving yourself and healing, you are setting the foundation;

❖ Remember... Everything is made up of energy. All matter including your physical body is made up of energy. Even your thoughts have energy;

❖ All power comes from within with a boost from the Divine Source when needed. Bring your awareness to the center of your head (between your ears and behind your eyes) and close your eyes... Take a few deep breaths. Breathe in through the nose for a count of four, hold the breath for four beats, and exhale for a count of four. Do this process four times;

❖ Ground yourself to the Earth's energies by imagining your root/base chakra having a connection to the Earth's core. Use your imagination to find a connection that works best for you;

❖ Clear your mind. Imagine everything that is in your mind being sent to the Earth to be grounded and cleansed. Use your imagination for your steps to do this. Be creative. There is no wrong way to do this;

❖ Quiet your mind. I find that pulling the blinds down in your mind helps. You may find a way that works better for you;

❖ You should feel very calm and peaceful now;

❖ We are all guided by the same life force energy. Ask to be filled where you need it most. Perhaps you have been pouring from an empty cup and have put yourself last. Fill yourself first by envisioning pure white healing energy filling your entire body, first starting at the crown of your head and into your neck, shoulders, hands, torso, legs, feet, and toes. Call the energy to the different parts of your body and tune into the sensations you are feeling and accept them;

❖ Accept Divine Love. You are worthy of love even if you have not or are not experiencing it in your waking life. If you are able, sit comfortably on the floor or ground with your palms facing downward and pressed into the earth. (If you can't do this then sit in a chair with your feet flat on the floor and your palms facing down on your thighs) Draw in a breath and hold for four seconds before releasing the breath and saying, "I accept Divine Love. I am worthy." Do this four times; and

❖ Sit in silence for 1-2 minutes (or more if you like) and enjoy the peace. When you are ready, gradually go back to your body, feel your body, be grateful, and open your eyes.

<u>Laughter therapy</u>

Laughter Therapy, also known as, Laughter Yoga is an alternative treatment that is considered a cognitive-behavioral therapy that has a positive effect on mental health and immune systems of those who practice it. Its healing properties have long been considered a placebo effect, yet the science is unmistakable. Laughter activates the neural pathways of emotions such as joy and it can improve your mood while helping to control brain levels of the neurotransmitter serotonin without using antidepressants.

Here are four ways that Laughter Therapy can help improve your health:

- ❖ Blood pressure – Studies show that when subjects were shown a sad movie, their blood pressure increased, but when shown a humorous movie, their blood pressure remained stable. Laughter therapy stimulates the parasympathetic nervous system;
- ❖ Immune function – Subjects exposed to a funny video for one hour showed an increase in immunoglobulins from blood samples that were taken before, during, and after the video was shown. The positive effects lasted for 12 hours!;
- ❖ Mental wellbeing – Laughter directly improves mood and helps lower stress levels. It has positive effects on physical health and relationships and can help with depression; and
- ❖ Blood sugar levels – Laughter can help moderate blood sugar levels after meals by reducing the marker prorenin and cause favourable changes in associated genetic markers such as diabetic nephropathy.

How to participate in Laughter Therapy:

- ❖ Add humour – Whether it's a movie, television show, funny video, or joke, find ways to add humour to your day;
- ❖ Find a group – Laughter Yogis are excellent guides in introducing you to Laughter Yoga. This type of therapy is done in a group setting where eye contact is maintained throughout between members who practice prolonged, voluntary laughter. This type of yoga is based on the belief that spontaneous laughter and voluntary laughter have the same benefits psychologically and physiologically; and
- ❖ Mirroring – This may be uncomfortable to do at first, but it will get easier and more enjoyable the more it's practiced. Stand in front of a mirror and maintain eye

contact with yourself. Mimic the funniest laugh you know, make funny faces, and try laughing in different pitches from low to high. You'll be laughing in no time once you get started!

A gentleman by the name of Norman Cousins discovered the real benefits of laughter therapy. He used laughter therapy to battle back from a deadly illness. "I made the joyous discovery that ten minutes of genuine belly laughter had an anesthetic effect and would give me at least two hours of pain-free sleep," he said. "When the pain-killing effect of the laughter wore off, we would switch on the motion picture projector again and not infrequently, it would lead to another pain-free interval."

There's another story of a woman, Saranne who was diagnosed with breast cancer and knew the benefits from Norman's story, so she decided to try laughter therapy just as he had; today she has helped countless others through laughter therapy that she calls 'Comedy Cures'.

Similar to laughter, the inner-smile has a beneficial effect on your wellbeing. The inner-smile, like laughter therapy, relieves stress and improves your mood.

Inner Smile

When you smile to your heart you create a loving energy that fills your entire body. Practicing the inner-smile improves the flow of energy (chi) along the meridians of the body and this results in improved health, vitality, and emotional and spiritual balance. Even at the cellular level there has been a noted improvement. Not only does your energy flow better, your brain is activated by the inner-smile and this causes the release of neurotransmitters such as dopamine and serotonin. When these are released, you will find that your body will relax, have a lower blood pressure, and improve your mental state. It isn't surprising that studies have found that people who smile live longer.

The Inner-Smile technique:

❖ Close your eyes;
❖ Feel grounded to the Earth's core;
❖ Use your imagination and find a happy place that makes you smile;
❖ Gently smile to your heart by curving the corners of your mouth slightly upward. You will feel your energy get lighter as you do this (you don't need a full on teeth showing smile but if it works for you then go for it);
❖ While gently smiling, feel your body fill with the positive energy;
❖ Be and feel grateful;
❖ Use your imagination and awareness to flow this healing energy to any and all parts of your body that need to relax, be nourished, or be refreshed; and
❖ Your body will give you feedback while you are focusing your energy on your body. You might feel heat, tingling, or light pressure.

A shorter version for quick balancing of charged emotions:

❖ Close your eyes;
❖ Ground yourself;
❖ Find your happy place;
❖ Smile gently to your heart;
❖ Let the energy flow until you feel lighter and at peace; and
❖ Be grateful for the blessing.

You will have a much better outcome during Reiki sessions or meditations if you maintain an inner-smile during the entire session. I would even recommend that you try the inner-smile technique throughout your day and journal the impact this has on your overall state of mind. Does this also change your perspective allowing you to see situations or solutions to challenges more clearly?

<u>A Healing Voice by Lacey L. Bakker</u>

I'd like to thank Lynn for including my story in her wonderful book and for her encouragement to share it.

Ever since I was a little girl, I was interested in the things that not everyone could see. I don't know how, but I knew and believed with every fiber of my being, that there was something bigger than me and that I could create my own reality. I'd do little tests like making it my intention to find a four-leaf clover or a fluffy white feather and much like pulling items out of thin air, they would appear. Over the years, I'd packed those intentions away to focus on my career, relationships, and family. My family has always known that there was something 'different' or 'special' about the things that I saw and heard that they couldn't. Sometimes it frightened them, so I decided to keep my experiences to myself. Years later, the Universe intervened when I needed it most and reminded me of its power and my own. This is my story.

In 2018 I suffered a grade two frontal lobe concussion from a snowmobile accident. I don't remember the accident itself, but I do remember what happened before and after. The after part was the most distressing.

According to the people I was with, I was unconscious for seven minutes. Waking up and not recognizing the people that surrounded me was scary, even though moments earlier I knew they were my friends. My mind was blank. Completely empty and black like a slate. The harder I tried to remember, the more terrified I became. I couldn't recall my name or what my work was and as I scanned my memory for answers, none came.

I was rushed to the hospital and seen within minutes where the doctor put my left shoulder back into its socket and ordered an MRI. Adrenaline rushed through my blood, and I vomited from the pain.

Another hospital. Another round of tests. No headache, no brain bleed. Light sensitivity set in quickly. I don't remember the details of what happened during that time.

I was sent home for rest, but little did I know that the aftereffects of my brain injury were about to rear their ugly heads. Nightmares, night terrors, and being scared to death to go to sleep because the images that filled my bruised brain were too much to bear.

The vertigo was so bad that I couldn't stand up. I crawled to the bathroom on my hands and knees and vomited all over the floor and myself. I crawled again to my bed and clung to the sheets as the whole world spun around me. The spinning would not stop. I made a plan to take my own life. There was no way I could live like this.

I attempted to get out of bed a second time to take the whole bottle of painkillers that I had been prescribed, but I could barely lift my head from the mattress.

As I lied in the darkness, I made a deal with the Universe. I begged it to just let me die. Those were my exact words. And in the blackness of my clenched eyes a whisper filled the room that said, *"You have too much left to do."*

The tears stopped and I opened my eyes. The world was still spinning, but something inside of me ignited. I decided right then and there that I could no longer allow a single negative thought into my mind. Doubt was too high of a price to pay in my recovery.

I dragged myself out of bed and on my hands and knees I slowly made it to the hallway. I grabbed the wall for support and steadied myself first on the floor and then against the doorframe. I took a shaky step, and then another.

Weeks passed and I attended therapy, chiropractor appointments, and appointments with my family physician. Slowly, I decided it was time for me to get outside.

It was the dead of winter and snow, and big chunks of ice lined the sidewalks. Getting dressed was a chore because of balance issues and the matter of my recently dislocated shoulder, but I was determined to get out of the house. The weight of my boots felt like bricks around my ankles and the ache in my brain was constant.

It took me two hours to walk around one city block in my neighbourhood. I shuffled and just kept putting one foot in front of the other. I don't know why I did what I did next, but I'm grateful that I did. Perhaps it was another sign from the Universe, the guidance that I so desperately needed to continue in my quest to keep getting better. I recorded myself, in my own voice on my phone and listened to it constantly. *Keep going, you can do this, you're doing great, you can do anything, you're strong, I'm proud of you, and you have too much left to do* is what I repeated over and over. I listened to my own voice, my own mantras, and the message from the Universe every day for six months.

Exactly one-hundred-and- ninety-seven days later, I felt like my old self again. Something inside me changed. I knew at that moment that the 'old me' had finally returned.

As horrific as my brain injury was, it needed to happen. It was supposed to happen. I needed to slow down. I needed to take care of myself for once. To put myself first.

The Universe saved my life that night with a quiet whisper to a tortured brain. The strength I needed to keep going lied within me and within the recording of my voice.

Creative Visualization and the Miracle Man

What do elite athletes, labouring mothers, and a comatose pilot have in common? They all practice creative visualization techniques to achieve their goals, heal their bodies, and train their minds to overcome massive challenges.

Creative visualization has helped people achieve health and wellness. Elite athletes put in thousands of hours of training to prepare for their sports and games, but they also spend hundreds of hours training in their minds. What the mind can conceive, the body can achieve. Perhaps you've heard of the Miracle Man, Morris Goodman, who recovered from a devastating plane crash that rendered him paralyzed, and unable to breathe, talk or swallow on his own.

Morris Goodman was flying his single engine plane around Chesapeake Bay; as he prepared to land, the engine lost power and fell through high-voltage power lines and flipped as it crashed into a field.

Doctors diagnosed Morris with a crushed spinal cord, crushed jaw and larynx, and a broken neck. He needed a tracheotomy because his diaphragm was almost destroyed, and he couldn't breathe on his own. He was connected to a respirator and his bladder, kidneys, and bowels were non-functioning. The doctors told Morris' family that he wouldn't make it through the night and that he would never walk, talk or move from the neck down and that he already beat the odds on the operating table when he went through nine hours of surgery to have his body stitched back together. But Morris had other plans. He believed so deeply that he would not only survive but thrive.

His recovery was painstakingly long. Each day he would listen to motivational speakers and follow their advice. One particular idea that stuck with Morris was a quote that said, *"When you turn on a light switch, you don't create electrical power. You release the power that is there all the time,"*- Zig Ziglar.

Morris knew the answer to his recovery was not on the outside, but that everything came from within him. He reached deep to summon the power that was inside of him. He began a secret program by himself that no doctor, nurse, or family member knew about; when the respirator took a breath for him, he would try to inhale 100 times in a row, then 200 and then 300 to train himself to breathe on his own again. He didn't tell anyone about his daily practices for fear of their discouragement and disbelief that he would ever heal. Two and a half months later, Morris was taken off the respirator.

He worked on relearning motor skills, eating solid food, and building strength from his hospital bed. Each day without fail, he visualized himself in perfect health, able to eat, breathe, talk, and walk on his own. He would visualize his legs moving one step at a time through the hallway and out the exit of the hospital.

Eight months later he walked out of the hospital, just like he visualized, on his own accord.

Creative visualization can also help with cleansing the chakras. Imagine pushing out or flushing blockages that are preventing the chakras from working at their optimum levels. You can visualize a swirling vortex of colour that matches the chakra that you are trying to unblock or a flower opening to its full potential and releasing the blockage. This is best done in a meditative state as with all creative visualization.

Some wonderful creative images to visualize can include:

- ❖ A waterfall washing over you and taking with it the pain or burdens you are experiencing;
- ❖ A drain with water swirling and swallowing the negativity or health issues you may be having; and
- ❖ A beam of light entering your crown chakra and flowing to the affected chakra related to the disease, allowing that energy to be healed in order to heal the physical disease related to it.

Whatever imagery you choose to hold in your mind and visualize is up to you. It should make you feel calm, at rest, and empowered.

You can choose to meditate in whichever way works best for you. Some people like to sit quietly, others prefer to be guided by audio or music, and some enjoy walking in nature as they meditate. Meditating helps to calm and quiet the mind and connects us to our inner knowledge, wisdom, and intuition. If there is an answer you seek, meditation may help you find it.

Meditations

For the meditations below you may record yourself saying the instructions. Use a soft and kind voice pausing to give yourself enough time at each step. You will figure the timing out as you practice. Eventually, you will know all the steps and can do the meditations without a voice guiding you. Listen to your favourite calming music and do the meditations or you may prefer to do the meditations in silence. Personally, I prefer to sit in silence doing my meditations. You will figure out, as you practice, what works best for you.

The body scan meditation covers many areas that may need healing. Please refer to Chapter 2, The Seven Chakras, where some illnesses or emotions related to the out of balance chakras are listed. If you find darkness in any of the chakra areas, then it may relate to one of the reasons for imbalance listed. If you don't see any darkness that is ok. Sensing or seeing comes in time. Just send the loving energy to your whole body and it will know what to do.

This meditation guides you to send the healing energies of unconditional love from the universe to the area in need of healing. It helps you to understand the source of the imbalance so that you can work on the mental and emotional aspects of the cause of the imbalance as well as have the healing energies help you through the healing process.

Body Scan Meditation

- ❖ Close your eyes;
- ❖ Smile gently;
- ❖ Ground yourself – see your root chakra connected to the center of the earth;
- ❖ Go into your mind and find your happy place;
- ❖ Clear out all the energies in your mind that are not useful and quiet your mind;
- ❖ Feel the peace of a clear and quiet mind;
- ❖ Call in the unconditionally loving and healing energies of the universe. You can call these in individually or you can simply call in all of the Loving Divine Energy of the Universe. Do what feels best for you and gets the loving energy flowing;
- ❖ Let these energies flow through you in the best possible way for the highest possible good. Feel the energy flowing through you. Feel the lightness. Feel the pure unconditional love;
- ❖ Use your awareness to scan your body;
- ❖ Start at your head and work your way down your body;
- ❖ Head, neck, shoulders, arms, chest, abdomen, pelvis,

thighs, knees, shins, feet, nape of the neck, upper back, middle back, lower back, buttocks, back of legs, back of thighs, calves, ankles, feet;

❖ Notice if there is any negative energy or shadow or dark spots that indicate the area needs healing energy sent to it;

❖ The healing energy is already flowing through your body so all you need to do is place your palm chakras over the place that needs healing, and the energy will flow out your palm chakras to the place in need of healing energy. If you cannot reach the place that needs the loving healing energy, then you can use your awareness and intention to send the energy from your palm chakras to the area that needs healing;

❖ You can also call on your healing angels or guardian angels to help you with difficult to reach places. Feel their healing hands as they help you send the loving energy to where it is needed. Feel their hands wipe away any energy cords that may be attached to your back or front of your torso that may have been attached throughout your day or week, sending love and forgiveness to the individual(s) who are responsible for the cords, and then releasing the cords to the earth to be cleansed. (These energy cords form for various reasons and make you feel tired and weak. It is a good practice to clear cords regularly.)

❖ Let the loving universal energy that is flowing through you, repair and fill the holes left by the cords and dark energy that were removed;

❖ Continue to bring in the healing energies of the universe and let it flow through you and around you. Be immersed in the loving energy;

❖ Be grateful that you have released all negative energies that are not useful and do not serve you well;

❖ Be grateful that you have replaced all negative energy with the unconditional love of the universe;

❖ Be grateful for any other blessings you may have received

today;
- ❖ You are now at peace;
- ❖ You are balanced;
- ❖ You are free;
- ❖ Go back to your body;
- ❖ Feel your body; and
- ❖ Open your eyes.

Tree meditation

During my Secrets of Natural Walking (SONW) practices I came up with this very grounding meditation. It feels wonderful connecting to the healing energies of the earth. This can be done anywhere - outside while walking or in your chair at work. It is relatively short timewise and really is lovely.

- ❖ Close your eyes;
- ❖ Smile gently;
- ❖ Ground yourself;
- ❖ Say the following to yourself:
- ❖ I am a tree...;
- ❖ I am nourished by the earth... (Feel the soil nourishing your roots);
- ❖ I am nourished by the air... (Feel the breeze gently moving your branches);
- ❖ I am nourished by the water... (Feel the water from the soil feeding your roots and the morning dew drops on your leaves);
- ❖ I am nourished by the fire... (Feel the warmth of the sun on your leaves);
- ❖ I am peace...;
- ❖ I am wisdom...;
- ❖ I am unconditional love...;
- ❖ I am grace...;
- ❖ I am patience...;

- ❖ I am harmony...;
- ❖ I am a tree...;
- ❖ Feel grateful;
- ❖ Go back to your body;
- ❖ Feel your body; and
- ❖ Open your eyes.

Being one with the universe or looking for answers

This exercise brings your body into the loving energies of the universe. Our soul is in our heart center or inner heart. The loving energy of the universe lives here at all times. With the loving universe energies in your heart center and being immersed in the loving energies, you will be and feel at one with everything. You will feel that entanglement at the quantum level.

As you are immersed in the unconditional love of the universe, you will feel like your body is sinking or compressing into the floor or chair and this is your body going into the theta brainwave state. You are at peace, surrounded in unconditional love, and can receive messages or get answers to questions that you may have. It is a great state to be in for self-love work and healing.

- ❖ Close your eyes;
- ❖ Smile gently;
- ❖ Ground yourself;
- ❖ Call on the loving and healing energies of Divine Source;
- ❖ Let Earth energies and Divine Source energies flow through you in the best possible way for the highest possible good;
- ❖ Feel yourself grounded and full of the energy of pure unconditional love;
- ❖ Let the loving Divine Source energies surround you and contain you so that you are fully immersed in the loving energies of Divine Source;

❖ Use your awareness and feel/sense that you are immersed in the loving energies of Divine Source and the loving energies of Divine Source are in you, in your inner heart. You are entangled. You are one;

❖ You may stop here if you are relieving some stress or anxiety. Sit in this unconditional love until the uneasy feelings subside. To finish, feel grateful, go back to your body, feel your body, and open your eyes;

❖ If you are looking for answers from your higher self or guides then continue;

❖ Open yourself to receive messages or answers to questions you may have;

❖ If you are receiving messages, just be open to any information that you may receive;

❖ If you are looking for answers to a question, first put the question out there in a loving way and then wait in your loving space for any form of answer. It may be a feeling, an image, or just a knowing or understanding;

❖ Remember to have no expectations and just let the energy flow;

❖ Be grateful for the information that you receive;

❖ Go back into your body;

❖ Feel your body; and

❖ Open your eyes.

Our intention creates our reality.
– Dr. Wayne Dyer

Intentions and Manifestation

Intentions are not the same as goals as they do not have expectations or evaluations. Clear intentions can guide our actions as we go about our day. Intentions are our hearts desires and setting our intentions bring our hearts and minds into alignment.

Intentions are what create our reality, what we imagine is what we become, and thoughts become things! Focusing our minds and hearts on our intention can help us bring it into reality.

Personal thoughts, values, and perspectives should be closely tied to our intentions that need to be clear and specific. It can be a simple word or phrase, such as love, strength, compassion, kindness for others, kindness for yourself, peace, and courage.

When setting intentions, keep them in a positive frame, instead of saying something like, "I don't want to be a coward," change it to, "I am courageous!"

To set your intention, ground yourself and get into a meditative state, if possible, with a few deep breaths before closing your eyes. Listen to your inner guidance and the guidance of Divine Source. Be sure to revisit your intention throughout the day. Call it to the center of your mind and visualize it and then release it into the Universe. Detach yourself from the outcome. It is also important that you are not the only person benefiting from your intention. The change in yourself should benefit those around you. You will be amazed at how the change in yourself has a ripple effect in those you interact with.

Examples of Intentions

Your intention should be something important and personal to you.

If your intention is to heal your body, mind, and soul, from trauma or situations you have experienced, you can say, I am healed. I forgive and release past hurts.

If your intention is to be more aware of your choices and how they will affect you and others, you can say, I think before acting. I listen to my inner wisdom to guide me to the perfect path.

If your intention is to be more empathetic, understanding, and patient with yourself and others, you can say, I am compassionate, patient, and unconditionally love others and myself. I give myself and others the time and space that they need to grow.

If your intention is to let go of the need to control people and situations you could say, I am free to let others be as they are and make their own decisions and to follow their beliefs. I am responsible for my actions, thoughts, and words.

If your intention is to be more aware of yourself, your intuition, your body, and inner wisdom you can say, I honour my feelings, my body, and my space. I allow all good things to come to me and I am thankful for my inner guidance which knows the best way to lead me.

If your intention is to be abundant, you can say, I am abundant. My life is full of wonderful experiences and people that are full of Joy. I am abundant in all aspects of my life.

If your intention is to be more loving and less judgmental, you can say, I lead with love and allow others to experience their own path of happiness.

The difference between Intention and Manifestation

Intention is the tool of conception. An intention is a seed that is planted, and manifestation is the flower. What you think about and intend has no choice but to manifest into your reality.

Manifestation is the tool of creation. It is the act of bringing about your thoughts into the physical world. Intention and manifestation work together. The two combined create the experiences that we wish to receive. Intention is the pathway in creating what we want to manifest, it's like shining a light on something that we wish to attract. If our intentions come from a place of love, positivity, joy, and enthusiasm, we reap the rewards, but if our intentions come from fear, that is what we'll create.

Lots of people believe that if they think thoughts of winning the lottery for example that it will happen, but that's not exactly how it works; manifestation is when we combine our intention, faith and belief that our intentions will come to fruition. But, if we have a seed of doubt that it's possible, we may not see the intention materialize. You may have set an intention, but if you've been doubting the reality of it manifesting, you've tainted the process, and nothing is created.

Manifestation can be halted by self-doubt, operating at a low frequency that is based in fear, and negative or mismatched thoughts. We attract circumstances, things, and conditions that are aligned with our consistent conscious and subconscious thoughts and beliefs.

We must focus on what serves us and what we want to attract with positivity. When we hold our intentions and make them clear, they become our habitual thoughts and desires and they have no choice but to manifest.

The Manifestation of this Book

My learning journey has been over a period of six years so far and is ongoing. The more you learn the more you learn how much there is to know. I never get tired of finding out the secrets kept from us. Each learning brings so much joy to my life and I feel freer with everything I am opened up to.

During my Reiki teachings I hit a bit of a roadblock. It was getting expensive to maintain my rate of learning and I wasn't comfortable relying on an organization that maintained their course costs when the pandemic hit. In 2020, when classes changed from in person to online, class sizes went from four or five in attendance at someone's home to nine hundred fifty or seven hundred fifty worldwide with live translation into six languages! The exchange of money for these courses rose more than exponentially. The courses are each $250.00 USD, and all of the courses are full days with the exception of the Kundalini and Meditation that are half days. I was flabbergasted at the profits of business behind the loving teachings and was assured that the profits do go towards local communities, the village fishermen, and other projects to help the less fortunate. This is as it should be for this industry and I am very happy to say that the Law of Giving and Receiving is in perfect balance.

Aside from the profits, the healing benefits of such a large group were astronomical. I had a bad wrist that was fully healed during my second weekend of online courses. Quite a phenomenal experience. The pain from the carpal tunnel affecting my left wrist was completely removed and never returned. The fascinating thing is that it was never the plan to heal my wrist during that weekend course. I noticed it afterwards and was very grateful for this blessing.

There are hundreds of Chakras in your body, and it was my goal to have Chakras one to seven (inside your body) and Shing Chi eight to twelve (outside your body) activated during my studies. I was able to get up to Shing Chi nine activated in my online classes by the Master Teacher. After my Reiki Tummo 3a level was taken online it was difficult to have my other Chakras activated. I was told that I had to take another course for each Chakra I wanted activated. After some research and much thought, I chose to try something different. I did some more research and realized everything I needed to continue my journey was available online AND in God's hands.

On YouTube you can find the attunements if you choose to go

that route, or you could just simply "Ask and it will be given to you". After you activate an out of body Chakra, my reiki organization told me that you need to work on connecting it to your Heart Chakra for ninety days in a row. If you miss a day, you must start over. I was very diligent and successful at this process. After connecting my Shing Chi ten Chakra to my heart, I asked God in my meditation if this is a necessary process for all the Chakras and then, suddenly, I felt intense energy coming down into my crown Chakra. After about what seemed like five or ten minutes, the force of the energy subsided and I felt like a whole different person. I felt whole and no longer shattered. My memory was infinitely improved and I had a very different understanding of the world and the people in it. It was like I could see things through a much clearer and less emotional lens. I realized that the structure I learned by previously is not the only way to evolve in the energy realm. That was a really great day! I am happy to say that all of my chakras were opened that day and connected to my heart chakra.

As I continued my learning, I realized that everyone should know about this. If you do not need a certificate to practice, then you can learn to heal yourself with the information available to you online. This is where the idea of this book was sparked. I've done the work and now I can share it with you. The manifestation of this book began.

I came up with a basic structure of the book and then expanded on each section. Every day I held the energy of how to write this book in the best possible way for the highest possible good.

The sections began to take form and as the book evolved other ideas emerged that made the book flow and transition better. I would have dreams at night and visions during the day for new additions. My vision for the cover came to me when I woke up one morning. Maybe it was a vision in a dream, and it was very powerful - helping people shatter the veil of negative energy that has them trapped in the darkness revealing the illuminated universe and unconditional love awaiting them on the other side. The person at their highest vibration is breaking out of the darkness. I knew this was the message I needed to share.

The dream of hearing a voice saying, "people need to be happier" was also a motivator. This was before the book cover vision, and it reinforced that I needed to get this information out as soon as possible. Happiness is deserved by all and helping people find happiness became my focus for several months as this book took on its own healing energy.

Even as I neared what I thought was the finish line I had new ideas pop into my head for the book. I hope that by the finish line I have brought in enough information for a holistic view and understanding of the universe that you were meant to discover.

What are your intentions and what do you want to manifest in your life?

Intention:

Live your life with intention
And use every ounce of your being
To live the life you were born to live.

\- Ana Brandt

_____

_____

_____

_____

_____

_____

_____

_____

_____

_____

_____

_____

_____

_____

_____

_____

_____

_____

_____

_____

_____

_____

_____

_____

_____

_____

_____

*If you commit to your
Intentions by taking aligned
Action, you will likely end
up Where you want to go.*
- christieinge.com

Intention is the beginning of all transformation.

\- unknown

_____

_____

_____

_____

_____

_____

_____

_____

_____

_____

_____

_____

_____

_____

_____

_____

_____

_____

_____

_____

_____

_____

_____

_____

An old day passes, a new day arrives.
The important thing is to make it meaningful.

\- Dalai Lama

10
CONTINUED LEARNING

Nature does not hurry, yet
Everything is accomplished.
– Lao Tzu

I've done a lot of research regarding healing energy, quantum physics, the laws of the universe, and energy codes and have spent many hours delving into different books about this subject matter and parallel ones. Some of the books I used in my learning journey are listed below for you if you are interested. Try letting your intuition guide you in your book selection from the list if you wish to explore these further.

My favourite books

The Law of One, 40th anniversary book set - by Ra, a humble messenger of The Law of One - Elkins Rueckett McCarty

The Gentle Way, book II, and book III - by Tom T Moore

Ho'oponopono the Hawaiian, forgiveness ritual as the key to your life's fulfillment - by Ulrich E Dupree

Universal Laws Unlocking the Secrets of the Universe, 7 Natural Laws of the Universe - by Creed McGregor

The Art of Peace - by Morihei Ushiba

The Energy Codes, the 7-step system to awaken your spirit, heal your body, and live your best life - by Dr Sue Mortimer

The Energies of Love, invisible keys to a fulfilling partnership - by Donna Eden & David Feinstein

The Way of the Monk, how to find purpose, balance, and lasting happiness - by Gaur Gopal Das

The Tapping Solution, a revolutionary system for stress free living - by Nick Ortner

Secrets of Aboriginal Healing, a physicist's journey with a remote Australian tribe - by Gary Holz with Robbie Holz

Aboriginal Secrets of Awakening, the other book - by Robbie Holz

The Holographic Universe - by Michael Talbot

The Tao of Physics - by Fritjof Capra

The Urantia Book, revealing the mysteries of God, The Universe, World History, Jesus, and ourselves - by the Urantia Foundation (authors unknown)

The Ascension Mysteries – by David Wilcock

The Synchronicity Key – by David Wilcock

The Source Field Investigations – by David Wilcock

Awakening in the Dream – by David Wilcock

Heart of the Sun, an anthology in exaltation of Sekhmet - edited by Candace C Kant and Anne Key

Great Decisions, Perfect Timing, cultivating intuitive intelligence - by Paul O'Brien

Theta Healing, introducing an extraordinary energy-healing modality - by Gianna Stibal

Advanced Theta Healing - by Gianna Stiba

Theta Healing Diseases and Disorders - by Gianna Stibal

The Essential Path - by Neale Donald Walsh

You Can Heal your Life - by Louise Hay

The Intuitive Awareness Method I AM - by Frederick Dodson

The Undiscovered Self - by C. G. Jung

Memories, Dreams, Reflections - by C. G. Jung

Synchronicity - by C. G. Jung

The "I AM" Disclosures - by Saint Germain Press

The Field - by Lynne McTaggart

The Silva Mind Control Method, by Jose Silva and Philip Miele
Activate Your Power - by Eitan Sharir

Secrets of Natural Walking - by Irmansyah Effendi

Reiki Tummo, An Effective Technique for Health and Happiness
- by Irmansyah Effendi

Education is not learning of facts,
but the training of the mind to think.
– Albert Einstein

Self Help

To assist you with your online searches for meditations and information for your healing journey I have included some of my most used search keywords and phrases. Once you get into your searches you will find other useful words to use in further searches. There are many groups on Facebook where you can get guidance from and many of them do free group healing sessions live on Facebook or Zoom. Explore as many sources as possible. Let your heart guide you - look inward and use your awareness to choose the options available to you. Your heart will always lovingly guide you on your learning journey.

You cannot control the results, only your actions.
— Allan Lokos

Best key words and phrases to start your search with for YouTube:

- ❖ Grounding meditation;
- ❖ Balance your chakra energy;
- ❖ Stress relief meditation;
- ❖ Energy boost meditation;
- ❖ Calming meditation;
- ❖ Sending energy to yourself;
- ❖ Looking for answers meditation;
- ❖ Open heart meditation; and
- ❖ Reiki Tummo.

I give my world permission to heal itself.
I allow all that is to be in alignment fully with its natural state
of abundance and harmony.
– unknown

Best key words and phrases to start your search with for Facebook:

- ❖ Meditation;
- ❖ Energy healing;
- ❖ Chakra balancing;
- ❖ Consciousness;
- ❖ Enlightenment;
- ❖ Vibrational healing;
- ❖ Shadow work; and
- ❖ Higher self.

While on YouTube and Facebook you will find websites related to the posts or videos and can grow your search from there. Let your higher self guide you to find the information that is right for you. Be aware of what you are watching (use your awareness) or listening to and sense if it is right for you.

> *Your actions are your only*
> *True belongings.*
> – Allan Lokos

Other sources of information on my learning journey:

❖ Gaia - I found many interesting shows and learning modules here;

❖ Mindvalley - I have the all-access pass membership and can take unlimited courses. A very cost-effective approach; and

❖ Natural Way of Living - this is where I learned Reiki Tummo. I have accessed the many free meditations on their website and on YouTube.

(Please note that I am not promoting the above organizations. I am merely stating that they were sources of information for me on my learning journey.)

A few more quotes to inspire you

> *I give my body permission to heal itself. I allow each cell to be*
> *in full alignment with its natural state of wellbeing.*
> - unknown

> *In the end, just three things matter:*
> *How well we have lived*
> *How well we have loved*
> *How well we have learned to let go*
> — Jack Kornfield

Patience is a form of wisdom. It demonstrates that we understand and accept the fact that sometimes things must unfold in their own time.
— Jon Kabat-Zinn

As above, so below.
To my higher self, I now
Surrender all control.

As without, so within.
Love will be my eternal
Mantra; my constant hymn.

As the universe, so the soul.
My heartbeat will match the
Beat of the universe; this
Being my lifetime goal.

May my body become the true
Embodiment of my soul. This
Is my affirmation; this will
Be my greatest manifestation.

-Jayson Yucha

ABOUT THE AUTHOR

Lynn H Baillie has her BSc in Mathematics and straight out of university she taught math at a private school and ran the tutoring center for all of the students. After getting married and having children she returned to the workforce. She chose to tutor math after hours and pursue the world of finance for her career and found her niche in the legal and compliance department. She took protecting the investor very seriously and made sure that the sales force behind the investments were in compliance with the rules, bylaws, and standards set by the regulators. Recently, Lynn found a new calling in the world of energy work and has been researching and practicing with much anticipation in helping as many people as possible find peace and abundance in their lives. There is no need to suffer, and the solution is already within you. Lynn is here to help you discover that.

www.ingramcontent.com/pod-product-compliance
Lightning Source LLC
Chambersburg PA
CBHW070331090426
42733CB00012B/2446

* 9 7 8 1 9 8 9 5 0 6 3 1 8 *